Remember them that are in bonds, as bound with them; and them which suffer adversity, as being yourselves also in the body.

Hebrews 13:3 KJV

Contents

Before You Start This Study

When Islamic State (ISIS) militants moved into northern Iraq, they began identifying Christian-owned property with the Arabic letter ن (*nun*) or "n" painted on homes, businesses, and churches. This single letter conveyed the powerful accusation that the occupants were people who followed Jesus of Nazareth rather than Islam. To be labeled "n" in a community dominated by Muslim extremists is a life-changing identity.

Any person who makes a faith commitment to Jesus, any person who chooses to be "n," pays a high cost. Without warning, some Christians have been dragged from their homes and businesses by armed militants and are never seen again. Pastors have been beheaded. Teenagers have been forced into service to ISIS or been raped, beaten, mutilated, and left for dead. Even young children who will not renounce Jesus have been shot. Once they are identified, Christians who refuse to convert to Islam must pay an excessively high tax, leave everything behind and flee, or die.

Since 2003 such persecution has forced more than a million Iraqi Christians who refuse to renounce Jesus and the Bible to flee their homes. Many of these survivors have escaped with nothing but the clothes on their backs. Often ISIS fighters at checkpoints along their escape routes have confiscated any material goods, money, identification, passports, food, and water Christians had managed to carry with them. In some cases family members, even children, have been taken.

Now these Christian survivors live in the tenuous safety of refugee camps scattered in safe-for-the-moment locations in cities and rural areas of Iraq, Turkey, Lebanon, and Jordan. They trust God daily for their food, shelter, and safety because they have no money, no options for finding work, and no other place to go. Even more challenging is the reality that their situation is not temporary. There is no expectation that their life circumstances will ever go back to "normal."

Yet their courageous, steadfast commitment to God in the face of persecution provides a powerful picture of what being "n" is all about. Their willingness to sacrifice everything they have in this world in order to fulfill God's calling to obey and serve him is inspiring. Like the heroes of the faith whose stories we read in the Bible and in the record of church history, they are living out Paul's words in Philippians 1:21: "For to me to live is Christ, and to die is gain."

Through this study series, we want you to get to know some of your brothers and sisters who are being persecuted for their Christian faith. We invite you to look deeply into their eyes and allow yourself to share in their experience of faith as they live it out in their world. It won't be easy. The circumstances they face truly are frightening. The experiences they endure are deeply painful.

Their stories aren't easy to "turn off" and forget, and they shouldn't be. Each of us who follows Jesus shares an identity with these persecuted people because we are members of the global family of Jesus Christ. Their stories matter because their stories are also our stories. As the family of Jesus on earth, we are drawn to embrace our suffering brothers and sisters and stand together—ministering to one another—as we seek to be instruments of God's grace in a desperately needy and hurting world.

Our goal in this study series is not to elicit pity for persecuted Jesus followers in hostile Muslim countries. Nor is this study intended to stimulate any hatred toward Muslims. God is doing a powerful work in the midst of the chaos and evil that is currently causing such upheaval in the Muslim world and beyond. Many followers of Jesus see in their moderate Muslim neighbors a deep hunger to know the truth about Jesus and the Bible. In response, they are eager to reach out to spiritually hungry Muslims and share the love and truth of Jesus—even when doing so may get them or their loved ones beaten, tortured, or killed.

Our intent for this study is simply to share the stories of persecuted Christians so you'll stand with them, care for them, encourage them, and pray for them. We dare not let them stand alone or suffer in silence. Our desire is for Christians around the world to recognize these persecuted followers of Jesus in the family of God and to embrace them in that intimate unity: "Remember them that are in bonds, as bound with them; and them which suffer adversity, as being yourselves also in the body" (Hebrews 13:3 KJV).

The Voice of the Martyrs

Sacrifice

And he said to all, "If anyone would come after me, let him
deny himself and take up his cross daily and follow me."

Luke 9:23

Session Start-Up

Sacrifice is never far from the hearts and minds of Christians who are persecuted by Islamic extremists. For our persecuted family in Jesus, the consequences of obeying Christ are clear. When these faithful believers choose Jesus as Lord and Savior, they count the cost of being his disciple. They know that once their faith becomes visible to others, persecution will follow. So they expect it and accept it.

The depth of the sacrifices they make in order to serve Christ faithfully is hard to comprehend if we haven't experienced such persecution. In many Muslim-controlled areas, Christians are forced out of their homes and communities. They are beaten and imprisoned. They are denied housing and turned down or fired from jobs. Some are sold as sex slaves or tortured. Others are beheaded in front of their children, who may then be persecuted.

Christian university students may be forced out of school, and administrators will delete all records of their attendance and accomplishments. Sometimes Islamic extremists murder entire families of believers.

Yet our Christian brothers and sisters in the Muslim world proclaim, through word and action, "It's worth it. We are disciples of Jesus. We will remain committed to God and his kingdom no matter what sacrifices are required. We are called to make disciples. No matter what happens, we have hope because Jesus promised to prepare a place for us where we will be with him forever!" Their sacrifices are a powerful testimony to our loving God whose grace reaches out to every sinner and who empowers those who receive Jesus as Savior and Lord to live in faithful service to him.

Through this video study session, we will see our persecuted family members up close and personal. We will gain insight into the sacrifices they make every day. We will explore what the Bible reveals about sacrifice in the life of Jesus and in the lives of those who follow him. May God open our eyes to see the world in which our brothers and sisters choose to be "living sacrifices" for Christ. May he open our hearts to love and stand with them wherever they live and serve.

Prayer

Dear Lord, as we begin this study together, we thank you for your enduring love for all people. We thank you for the opportunity we have to worship and serve you. Please open our eyes and hearts to see the world in which our persecuted brothers and sisters in

Christ live. Help us to understand more fully the challenges they face and the sacrifices they make in order to follow you faithfully. Help us to see them not only from our human perspective but as you see them; to see their role in advancing your kingdom and to embrace them as our true family in Christ. In the name of Jesus we pray, amen.

Video Exploration
Video Notes

> Jesus said persecution would come
> What it means to lose everything
> People are open to Jesus
> Choosing to stay and suffer
> God is taking care of us

Video Discussion

1. When you see and hear about the suffering these Christians endure for the sake of Jesus, what is your response when you hear them say, "No one cares"?

2. Many Christians in northern Iraq were teachers, professionals, and businesspeople who lived reasonably comfortable lives before the war and before ISIS. Now they find themselves without a home, without any money, with no clothing other than what they are wearing, without food or water, with no options for finding work, and often no opportunity to move to a better place.

What are your thoughts as you try to put yourself in their situation?

How different are their lives from the life you thought you "signed up" for when you became a Christian?

3. As you consider what the people interviewed in the video say about their situation and how they choose to live for Jesus, what do you think it takes—in terms of belief, experiences, faith commitment—for people to make such great sacrifices to stand firm in their faith in Jesus?

4. It is easy to see the news of what is happening in Iraq and Syria and yet be disconnected from the real horror of what is taking place and the people who are living those experiences.

What did this video help you to realize about the expansion of ISIS in the region (northeastern Syria and northern Iraq)?

In what way has this video helped to connect you with the people who are your persecuted family in Christ?

How do you now feel differently about the Christians to whom you have been introduced?

5. In what ways have the testimonies of believers highlighted in this video challenged or encouraged you to live out your faith in your world?

Fact File: I Am N

As stated earlier, when Islamic State (ISIS) militants moved into northern Iraq, they began identifying Christian-owned property. Families would find the Arabic letter ن (*nun*) or "n" painted on their homes, businesses, and churches. This single letter conveyed the powerful accusation that the occupants were "Nazarenes," people who followed Jesus of Nazareth rather than Islam.

To be labeled "n" in a community dominated by Muslim extremists is a life-changing identity. With this mark comes the ultimatum: "If you convert to Islam or pay the tax, you can keep your material possessions and remain in this community. If not, leave or you will die." Any person who takes a stand for Jesus in ISIS-occupied Iraq, any person who chooses to be "n," pays a high cost.

> Without warning, some Christians are dragged from their homes and businesses by armed militants—and they are never seen again.
>
> Pastors who share the message of Jesus in their communities are beheaded in front of their families.
>
> Children who will not renounce Jesus may be shot.
>
> Teenagers may be taken from their homes and families and forced into service to ISIS or raped, beaten, mutilated, and left for dead.
>
> Other atrocities are so horrific we will not describe them here.

Since 2003, such persecution has forced more than a million Iraqi Christians who refuse to renounce Jesus and the Bible to flee their homes. Many of these survivors have escaped with nothing but the clothes on their backs. At checkpoints along the way, ISIS fighters have confiscated any material goods, money, identification, passports, food, and water that Christians had managed to carry with them. In some cases family members, even young children, were taken away.

Now these Christians live in the tenuous safety of refugee camps. They trust God daily for their food, shelter, and safety because they have no money, no options for finding work, and no other place to go. Even more challenging is the reality that their situation is not temporary; their life circumstances are unlikely to improve in the foreseeable future.

Yet their courageous, steadfast commitment to God in the face of persecution provides a powerful picture of what being "n" is all about. They willingly sacrifice everything they have in this world in order to fulfill God's calling to obey and serve him. Like the heroes of the faith whose stories we read in the Bible and in the record of church history, they are living out Paul's words in Philippians 1:21: "For to me to live is Christ, and to die is gain."

Bible Perspective

People all over the world, those who know Jesus as well as those who do not, are willing and able to make some sacrifices. We will, for example, sacrifice for people we love and for causes that concern us deeply. But from a human perspective, we are careful about the sacrifices we make. We make sacrifices that we deem worthwhile, that have a positive outcome for us. If we consider a sacrifice to be too costly, we choose not to make it. So what is the basis for sacrificing everything—home, career, material goods, even one's life—in order to stand with Jesus?

1. The Bible challenges everyone who chooses to follow Jesus to walk in the same way Jesus walked (1 John 2:6). Consider each of the following passages and discuss two things: 1) the sacrifices Jesus made in order to fulfill God's purpose for his life on earth; 2) the ways the sacrifices made by persecuted Christians today reflect the sacrifices he made.

a. "Then the soldiers of the governor took Jesus into the governor's headquarters, and they gathered the whole battalion before him. And they stripped him and put a scarlet robe on him, and twisting together a crown of thorns, they put it on his head and put a reed in his right hand. And kneeling before him, they mocked him, saying, 'Hail, King of the Jews!' And they spit on him and took the reed and struck him on the head. And when they had mocked him, they stripped him of the robe and put his own clothes on him and led him away to crucify him" (Matthew 27:27–31).

b. "Now the men who were holding Jesus in custody were mocking him as they beat him. They also blindfolded him and kept asking him, 'Prophesy! Who is it that struck you?' And they said many other things against him, blaspheming him" (Luke 22:63–65).

c. "And with him they crucified two robbers, one on his right and one on his left. And those who passed by derided him, wagging their heads and saying, 'Aha! You who would destroy the temple and rebuild it in three days, save yourself, and come down from the cross!' So also the chief priests with the scribes mocked him to one another, saying, 'He saved others; he cannot save himself. Let the Christ, the King of Israel, come down now from the cross that we may see and believe.' Those who were crucified with him also reviled him" (Mark 15:27–32).

d. "For you know the grace of our Lord Jesus Christ, that though he was rich, yet for your sake he became poor, so that you by his poverty might become rich" (2 Corinthians 8:9).

e. "Have this mind among yourselves, which is yours in Christ Jesus, who, though he was in the form of God, did not count equality with God a thing to be grasped, but emptied himself, by taking the form of a servant, being born in the likeness of men. And being found in human form, he humbled himself by becoming obedient to the point of death, even death on a cross" (Philippians 2:5–8).

2. In what ways has the video you have just seen been a practical demonstration of the meaning of Romans 12:1: "I appeal to you therefore, brothers, by the mercies of God, to present your bodies as a living sacrifice, holy and acceptable to God, which is your spiritual worship"?

3. Read 1 Peter 2:21–23: "For to this you have been called, because Christ also suffered for you, leaving you an example, so that you

might follow in his steps. He committed no sin, neither was deceit found in his mouth. When he was reviled, he did not revile in return; when he suffered, he did not threaten, but continued entrusting himself to him who judges justly."

In what ways are your persecuted Christian brothers and sisters living out this perspective, and how does their example speak to you?

What do these verses teach you about how to respond to the persecution—ridicule, rejection, retaliation—you may experience in life because of your faith in Jesus?

If you feel comfortable doing so, share what changes you need to make in your walk of faith in order to more fully live out Christ's calling.

4. From a human perspective, those who persecute and harm followers of Jesus tend to view their "victims" as inferior, weak, helpless, and far less valuable than themselves. But God's perspective is quite different. Read Luke 21:10–17 and John 16:1–3, taking note of how Jesus presents an inverted perspective on who has the real power when it comes to being persecuted for the sake of Christ.

> Then he said to them, "Nation will rise against
> nation, and kingdom against kingdom. There
> will be great earthquakes, and in various places
> famines and pestilences. And there will be terrors

and great signs from heaven. But before all this they will lay their hands on you and persecute you, delivering you up to the synagogues and prisons, and you will be brought before kings and governors for my name's sake. This will be your opportunity to bear witness. Settle it therefore in your minds not to meditate beforehand how to answer, for I will give you a mouth and wisdom, which none of your adversaries will be able to withstand or contradict. You will be delivered up even by parents and brothers and relatives and friends, and some of you they will put to death. You will be hated by all for my name's sake." (Luke 21:10–17)

I have said all these things to you to keep you from falling away. They will put you out of the synagogues. Indeed, the hour is coming when whoever kills you will think he is offering service to God. And they will do these things because they have not known the Father, nor me. (John 16:1–3)

What assurance, promises, and power does Jesus provide for believers who choose the sacrifice of persecution for his name?

Based on these verses, what opportunities does persecution provide for followers of Jesus, and how do you respond to that?

How does the empowerment of Christ affect believers who face persecution, and in what ways did you see this demonstrated in the video?

> The persecuted church, ultimately, is not a church of victims! If faithful to Scripture, they go forth in the power of God, believing that suffering is not the worst thing that can happen to them.
>
> Glenn M. Penner

Our Response

We know that throughout history God's people have suffered persecution and have made great sacrifices to stand for Jesus, but it can be difficult to "connect" what has happened in history with our everyday lives. What we have seen today is in some ways a replay of what we read about in the Bible, yet it is very real; it is happening right now. It is about our world, our times, our brothers and sisters who we can see, touch, and talk with. They are actually doing it!

What impact does their eagerness to sacrifice so much for Jesus have on you?

What action does their enthusiastic sacrifice challenge you to do?

First Corinthians 12:12–18, 25–26 provides a picture of our responsibilities concerning our persecuted family members in Christ throughout the world:

For just as the body is one and has many members, and all the members of the body, though many, are one body, so it is with Christ. For in one Spirit we were all baptized into one body—Jews or Greeks, slaves or free—and all were made to drink of one Spirit.

For the body does not consist of one member but of many. If the foot should say, "Because I am not a hand, I do not belong to the body," that would not make it any less a part of the body. And if the ear should say, "Because I am not an eye, I do not belong to the body," that would not make it any less a part of the body. If the whole body were an eye, where would be the sense of hearing? If the whole body were an ear, where would be the sense of smell? But as it is, God arranged the members in the body, each one of them, as he chose … that there may be no division in the body, but that the members may have the same care for one another. If one member suffers, all suffer together; if one member is honored, all rejoice together.

When Jesus followers we know—in our neighborhoods, workplaces, communities—experience times of hardship or sacrifice, we often step in to provide encouragement, help, and prayer. What are some of the ways we can do this for our persecuted family in Christ?

Some of the Christians featured in the video believe with all their heart that God will take care of them no matter what. As a result, they enthusiastically sacrifice everything they have to stand for him. As believers who do not now suffer in the same way they do, what is our responsibility to them? What do you think it looks like to suffer with them and to care for them as part of the same body?

The Christians in the video probably weren't expecting their lives to be as they are now. But they are certain their lives belong to God so they are willing to give it all. How do their examples inspire you in your walk with God? Encourage you to know him fully and follow him eagerly?

Closing Prayer

Let us join our hearts together before God and pray for the body of Christ. Let us begin our prayer together, then continue with individual prayers as each of us is led, until we close.

Dear Lord, we gather before you to pray for our brothers and sisters in Christ who are facing such severe persecution … [prayers of the group] … We are blessed by their eagerness to sacrifice everything and stand for you. We pray that they will be comforted in their sufferings and will know that they do not suffer alone. In Jesus's name we pray, amen.

Next Steps
God Is Taking Care of Us!

Jesus has promised great reward to those who sacrifice and suffer for the sake of his name. Over and over again, our Christian brothers and sisters who sacrifice so much for the sake of Christ remind us that God is taking care of them—even in the midst of great difficulties and hardship.

That knowledge and confident trust that God is taking care of them today and will take care of them for eternity spurs them on to even greater faithfulness and sacrifice. It is what prompts Aram to say, "Nothing can stop me from what I'm doing because I know that he's protecting me." It prompts Pastor Karim to say, "We experienced in these six months too many of God's promises. He's taking care of every single thing."

The choice to sacrifice everything for Jesus comes down to one very big question: Do I honestly believe Christ is alive, taking care of me today and waiting for me in heaven? Consider what Jesus himself has said about those who are persecuted for his sake and what they can expect from his hand.

> Blessed are those who are persecuted for righteousness' sake, for theirs is the kingdom of heaven.
>
> Blessed are you when others revile you and persecute you and utter all kinds of evil against you falsely on my account. Rejoice and be glad, for your reward is great in heaven, for so they persecuted the prophets who were before you. (Matthew 5:10–12)
>
> And he said to them, "Truly, I say to you, there is no one who has left house or wife or brothers or parents or children, for the sake of the kingdom of God, who

will not receive many times more in this time, and in the age to come eternal life." (Luke 18:29–30)

Blessed are you when people hate you and when they exclude you and revile you and spurn your name as evil, on account of the Son of Man! Rejoice in that day, and leap for joy, for behold, your reward is great in heaven; for so their fathers did to the prophets. (Luke 6:22–23)

Whoever finds his life will lose it, and whoever loses his life for my sake will find it. (Matthew 10:39)

And everyone who has left houses or brothers or sisters or father or mother or children or lands, for my name's sake, will receive a hundredfold and will inherit eternal life. (Matthew 19:29)

What encouragement do you see these passages of Scripture providing for your Christian brothers and sisters who currently endure great suffering because they stand with Jesus?

What impact do these passages of Scripture have on you and your willingness to make personal sacrifices when you face opposition for standing firm in your faith? Be specific.

By our sacrifice, God will tear the Islamic curtain and show the real face of Islam. Everything is possible for God to change, if we are ready for His will to be done in and through our lives, even to the death.

Narsbek, Kyrgyzstan

Courage

*Be sober-minded; be watchful. Your adversary the devil prowls
around like a roaring lion, seeking someone to devour. Resist
him, firm in your faith, knowing that the same kinds of
suffering are being experienced by your brotherhood throughout
the world. And after you have suffered a little while, the God
of all grace, who has called you to his eternal glory in Christ,
will himself restore, confirm, strengthen, and establish you.*

1 Peter 5:8–10

Session Start-Up

The magnitude of the suffering endured by Christians, as well as people of other religious minorities, who once lived in ISIS-controlled areas of Syria and Iraq is overwhelming. It is truly terrifying. The depravity of the persecution they experience is more than our minds can comprehend, the brutality more than our hearts can bear.

But since the earliest Bible times, God has called people to serve him in the midst of grave danger and seemingly impossible circumstances. So what enables a person to stand for Jesus in the midst of what is happening in Syria and Iraq today? What releases a person from paralyzing fear to follow Jesus faithfully no matter what?

Through this video study session, we will meet some courageous Christians. They aren't courageous because of their positive thinking or confidence in their own strength. They are people just like us who face a powerful enemy—an enemy using every tool at his disposal to destroy and kill God's people and hinder their spiritual activities. Human courage alone is insufficient to fight this battle. It cannot motivate a person in ISIS-controlled territory to share the gospel with a Muslim neighbor, participate in a house church, distribute Bibles, or lead clandestine Bible studies for new believers.

These brothers and sisters in Christ have the courage to stand for Jesus and face persecution only because their faith is rooted in the knowledge that God is at work in and through them to accomplish his will. Their perspective on life extends beyond what is happening to them here on earth to the eternity God promises to those who belong to him. Their courage is nurtured by the promise that God is with them and will never leave them. Confident of God's power and presence with them, they draw strength to stand against insurmountable odds. Let's see what we can learn about courage that leads to bold action despite the risks of life-threatening chaos.

Prayer

Heavenly Father, we have gathered together to get to know some of our brothers and sisters in Christ who face severe persecution for following you. Open our eyes to see and understand what you want us to experience. Open our hearts to care deeply for our persecuted family—to share in their fear, pain, uncertainty—not so that we will be afraid, but so that we will stand with them and support them in meaningful ways. Prepare us also to stand courageously for you in our world. In Jesus's name we pray, amen.

Video Exploration
Video Notes

> When ISIS comes
>
> Christians in the bull's-eye of persecution
>
> The light of Jesus in darkness and sorrow
>
> Courage to do what is not easy

Video Discussion

1. The video we have seen paints a graphic, but very real, picture of what our Christian brothers and sisters are suffering in Syria and Iraq. As you consider the widespread suffering and extreme brutality these Christians endure, what are your thoughts?

What questions do their experiences raise?

What do you struggle to comprehend?

2. For a moment, let's try to put ourselves into the chaos and terror our persecuted family experiences when ISIS takes over their cities and villages.

What do you think would be your greatest concerns?

How might such a crisis affect your spiritual convictions, your thoughts, your actions?

What stands out in your mind about how your Christian brothers and sisters face and respond to these circumstances?

3. What do you notice about people who have survived all of this—being shot, being kidnapped and chained, having their teeth knocked out—who still stay, who still pastor, who still tell others about Jesus, who still give Bibles to anyone who wants them?

4. The natural human response to the horrors and atrocities ordinary people face from the threat of ISIS is paralyzing fear. What seems to give these believers the courage to move forward in obedience to Jesus?

5. What do you think the pastor meant when he stated, "If we don't believe, Christianity is a very hard religion," and in what ways would you agree or disagree?

Displaced People of the Islamic State Campaign

Persecution is not new for Christians who have lived in Syria and Iraq, but the rise of ISIS, the Islamic State insurgency (referred to as *Da'esh* by some), has been a game changer. A self-proclaimed global caliphate, ISIS claims religious, political, and military authority over Muslims worldwide. The extreme violence and brutality of the ISIS takeover in Syria and Iraq is changing life for Christians, other religious minorities, and even Muslims.

Syria historically has been a secular state where Islam is recognized as the majority religion. It has been home to diverse ethnic and religious groups including Kurds, Armenians, Assyrians, Christians, Druze, Alawites, as well as Shiite and Sunni Muslims. The civil war that began in March 2011 dramatically changed the climate for all Syrians, including Christians who formerly had relative freedom within the larger Islamic society. Hundreds of thousands of Syrians have been killed; millions have been displaced internally or have fled the country.

The difficulty of life in Syria adds fuel to the exodus. Food and medicine are in short supply. Electricity, if available, may be on for only a few hours a day. Travel is dangerous because multiple armed factions establish checkpoints wherever they please. In some historically Christian communities where Muslims and Christians have lived in harmony for years, radical Islamist militias such as Al Nusra Front (an al-Qaida affiliate) have taken over. Their presence has displaced not only longtime residents, but families that had been forced to flee other areas of Syria and for a short time found refuge in these towns.

Prior to 2003, 1.5 million Christians lived in Iraq, their population concentrated in the northern part of the country known as the Nineveh Plains. But since the Iraq war ended in 2011, Iraq has struggled to achieve political and economic stability, resulting in a complicated situation where Christians may be severely persecuted or have relative freedom to practice their faith.

In June 2014, ISIS seized control of Mosul, Iraq's second-largest city, forcing nearly all of its thirty-five thousand Christians to flee. As the summer progressed, ISIS continued its advance. Approximately two hundred thousand Christians fled the cities and villages of the Nineveh Plains, which had been home for Christians for nearly two thousand years. In early 2015, ISIS began kidnapping Christians from villages in northeastern Syria and expelled Christians from the ancient city of Palmyra in central Syria.

The instability and conflict in Syria and Iraq during recent years has forced hundreds of thousands of people—Christians, other religious minorities, and Muslims who fear for the safety of their families—to flee to Jordan, Lebanon, Turkey, and the semi-autonomous Kurdistan region in northeast Iraq. The continued rise of ISIS has added hundreds of thousands to their numbers.

Life for these refugees is extremely difficult. They often lack even the basic necessities of shelter and food. But God is working mightily in the midst of the suffering and chaos. Christians are standing boldly for Christ, at times providing practical assistance for their Muslim neighbors and risking their lives to share the message of God's love with them. Many Muslim people, appalled by the brutality of Islamic extremists, are showing sincere interest in reading the Bible and learning about Jesus.

Bible Perspective

Courage to stand for Jesus in the climate in which persecuted Christians live cannot be based on human strength or emotion, on getting "pumped up" for the faith. Courage that counters the fear of the threats Christians in Iraq and Syria face results from a total commitment to obediently serve God and pursue his will. Such commitment grows out of a personal relationship with God—the knowledge, belief, and experience that reveals God to be powerful and trustworthy in all of his promises. Let's explore what the Bible says about fear and courage in the hearts of those who take the risk of standing for Jesus.

1. God knows the risks and dangers of faithful obedience to him, and throughout the Bible we read promises that he will be with his people during such times. God made one of those promises when Moses commissioned the Israelites to take possession of the Promised Land under Joshua's leadership: "Be strong and courageous. Do not fear or be in dread of them, for it is the LORD your God who goes with you. He will not leave you or forsake you" (Deuteronomy 31:6).

> When we face persecution, what role does our trust in God's promises and our awareness of his presence with us play in dealing with our fear and giving us courage?

2. Jesus knew that if his followers faithfully obeyed his command to make disciples, they would suffer the kind of opposition and persecution that induces fear. So he said:

> Do not fear those who kill the body but cannot kill the soul. Rather fear him who can destroy both soul and body in hell. Are not two sparrows sold for a penny? And not one of them will fall

to the ground apart from your Father. But even the hairs of your head are all numbered. Fear not, therefore; you are of more value than many sparrows. So everyone who acknowledges me before men, I also will acknowledge before my Father who is in heaven, but whoever denies me before men, I also will deny before my Father who is in heaven. (Matthew 10:28–33)

How valuable in God's sight is everyone who honors him, and how much does he care for each of us even when we can't see him at work on our behalf?

What difference does his watchful care over us make when we are fearful?

3. Not only does the Bible teach us to not be afraid when we suffer hardship in living out our faith, it gives us reason to hope:

Blessed be the God and Father of our Lord Jesus Christ! According to his great mercy, he has caused us to be born again to a living hope through the resurrection of Jesus Christ from the dead, to an inheritance that is imperishable, undefiled, and unfading, kept in heaven for you, who by God's power are being guarded through faith for a salvation ready to be revealed in the last time. In this you rejoice, though now for a little while, if necessary,

you have been grieved by various trials, so that the
tested genuineness of your faith—more precious
than gold that perishes though it is tested by fire—
may be found to result in praise and glory and honor
at the revelation of Jesus Christ. (1 Peter 1:3–7)

What is the living hope we have as Christians, and what difference
did you see that hope make in the lives of believers in the video?

In what ways does their example move us toward a greater
awareness of and dependence on God's Word, and how does this
strengthen our courage?

4. Persecutors can be very effective at stripping away our value as
human beings, in convincing us that we are alone, that we don't
matter, and that no one cares about us. In contrast, Romans 8:35–39
presents a different picture of our value in Christ:

Who shall separate us from the love of Christ? Shall
tribulation, or distress, or persecution, or famine,
or nakedness, or danger, or sword? As it is written,

"For your sake we are being killed all the day long;
we are regarded as sheep to be slaughtered."

No, in all these things we are more than con-
querors through him who loved us. For I am sure
that neither death nor life, nor angels nor rulers,

nor things present nor things to come, nor pow-
ers, nor height nor depth, nor anything else in all
creation, will be able to separate us from the love of
God in Christ Jesus our Lord.

How relevant is this passage to the persecution Christians are
enduring in the world today, and what do you think it means to
them in light of what they experience every day?

What empowerment does the promise of God's love give us as
we seek to be faithful and courageous in serving Jesus?

5. In his letter to the Philippians, Paul encourages believers to
fight for the sake of the gospel message, knowing that it will take
courage to do so: "Only let your manner of life be worthy of
the gospel of Christ, so that whether I come and see you or am
absent, I may hear of you that you are standing firm in one spirit,
with one mind striving side by side for the faith of the gospel, and
not frightened in anything by your opponents. This is a clear sign
to them of their destruction, but of your salvation, and that from
God. For it has been granted to you that for the sake of Christ
you should not only believe in him but also suffer for his sake"
(Philippians 1:27-29).

When God's people stand firm and fearlessly live out the gospel
of Christ even when they suffer, what message does that send to
their persecutors?

In what ways are persecuted Christians in the Muslim world actually seeing this happen, and how does it affect them? How does it affect you?

6. It is easy to be overwhelmed by fear when we can't see beyond the suffering persecution brings. Isaiah 26:3–4 presents an alternate focus: "You keep him in perfect peace whose mind is stayed on you, because he trusts in you. Trust in the LORD forever, for the LORD GOD is an everlasting rock."

What does Isaiah say will bring peace to our minds and hearts?

How does focusing our thoughts on the Lord and trusting in him give us courage when we are afraid? What examples have you seen of this in the video? In your own life?

> I don't think about the risks and the dangers. I think about Christ.
>
> Syrian pastor

Our Response

We may not face life-threatening persecution in our daily lives, but we still face persecution. It often comes in the form of mockery, bigotry, insults, injustice, bullying, and false accusations. It is painful and scary to be humiliated and rejected by people who oppose us because of our faith. Just as our persecuted brothers and sisters need courage in order to live for Christ in their world, we need courage to walk faithfully with Jesus and to share his message boldly instead of hiding in fear.

As you seek to walk with Jesus, which situations cause you to be fearful or to question whether or not you should stand firm in what you believe?

What have you discovered thus far in this session, either from your persecuted brothers and sisters in Christ or from the Bible passages we have explored, that strengthens your courage or changes how you think about what it means to live as a faithful follower of Jesus?

Much of the video you have seen was recorded when representatives from The Voice of the Martyrs went into Iraq to deliver supplies to the Christian refugees there. How do you think their courage, as Westerners traveling near ISIS-controlled areas and being questioned by security police, was tested?

Why do you think it was important for them to go despite the risks they faced?

As David, whom God chose to become king of Israel, tried to fulfill God's will for his life, he faced many powerful enemies and life-threatening situations. He had many opportunities to be afraid and to lose courage for the task God had put before him. The following psalm by David gives us an idea of how he found courage to be faithful. Let's read it aloud together:

The LORD is my light and my salvation;
 whom shall I fear?
The LORD is the stronghold of my life;
 of whom shall I be afraid?

When evildoers assail me
 to eat up my flesh,
my adversaries and foes,
 it is they who stumble and fall.

Though an army encamp against me,
 my heart shall not fear;
though war arise against me,
 yet I will be confident.

One thing have I asked of the LORD,
 that will I seek after:
that I may dwell in the house of the LORD
 all the days of my life,
to gaze upon the beauty of the LORD
 and to inquire in his temple. (Psalm 27:1–4)

What in this psalm strengthens your courage and likely the courage of your persecuted family in Iraq and Syria?

The persecuted family of Jesus has always needed the prayers and support of their fellow believers. Second Thessalonians 3:1–3 reminds us how important our prayers for one another are: "Finally, brothers, pray for us, that the word of the Lord may speed ahead and be honored, as happened among you, and that we may be delivered from wicked and evil men. For not all have faith. But the Lord is faithful. He will establish you and guard you against the evil one."

What is our commitment to make this our prayer for one another and for our persecuted brothers and sisters around the world?

Closing Prayer

Let us close our time together in prayer.

Dear Lord, we thank you for your love that redeemed us and for your watchful care over us in all circumstances. We could not have the courage to walk faithfully through persecution if you were not with us. Please help us to stand courageously for you wherever we are. We lift up our persecuted family throughout the world and ask you to provide wisdom, faithfulness, protection, courage, peace, and hope as they boldly stand for you in hostile places. Before you, we commit to pray for them regularly, asking you to empower them by your Spirit to be your witnesses. May all of us be united together to know you, trust you, and serve you faithfully no matter what the cost. In Jesus's name we pray, amen.

Next Steps
Not Ashamed to Serve

While the Jewish people were in captivity in Babylon, the king made a golden image of himself and required everyone to bow down before it and worship him. Some of the Jews, who had been placed in ruling positions in Babylon, were determined to faithfully obey God even while in captivity and refused to worship the king's image or serve his gods. This is where we pick up their story in Daniel 3:14–15:

> Nebuchadnezzar answered and said to them, "Is it true, O Shadrach, Meshach, and Abednego, that you do not serve my gods or worship the golden image that I have set up? Now if you are ready when you hear the sound of the horn, pipe, lyre, trigon, harp, bagpipe, and every kind of music, to fall down and worship the image that I have made, well and good. But if you do not worship, you shall immediately be cast into a burning fiery furnace. And who is the god who will deliver you out of my hands?"

The three men answered that they could serve and worship only their God. They also testified that their God would deliver them from the furnace, and that even if he didn't, they would not worship the king's gods or his statue. This infuriated the king:

> Then Nebuchadnezzar was filled with fury, and the expression of his face was changed against Shadrach, Meshach, and Abednego. He ordered the furnace heated seven times more than it was usually heated. And he ordered some of the mighty men of his army to bind Shadrach, Meshach, and

Abednego, and to cast them into the burning fiery
furnace. (Daniel 3:19–20)

The furnace was so hot that it killed the soldiers who threw
Shadrach, Meshach, and Abednego into it. But then an amazing
miracle occurred:

> Then King Nebuchadnezzar was astonished and
> rose up in haste. He declared to his counselors,
> "Did we not cast three men bound into the fire?"
> They answered and said to the king, "True, O
> king." He answered and said, "But I see four men
> unbound, walking in the midst of the fire, and they
> are not hurt; and the appearance of the fourth is
> like a son of the gods."
>
> Then Nebuchadnezzar came near to the door of
> the burning fiery furnace; he declared, "Shadrach,
> Meshach, and Abednego, servants of the Most High
> God, come out, and come here!" Then Shadrach,
> Meshach, and Abednego came out from the fire.
> And the satraps, the prefects, the governors, and the
> king's counselors gathered together and saw that the
> fire had not had any power over the bodies of those
> men. The hair of their heads was not singed, their
> cloaks were not harmed, and no smell of fire had
> come upon them. Nebuchadnezzar answered and
> said, "Blessed be the God of Shadrach, Meshach,
> and Abednego, who has sent his angel and delivered

his servants, who trusted in him, and set aside the king's command, and yielded up their bodies rather than serve and worship any god except their own God." (Daniel 3:24–28)

What does this story say to you about courage to serve God at all costs and God's power to deliver from harm those who serve him?

What impact did their faithfulness have on their king and his knowledge of God?

In what ways is this similar to what is happening among some Muslims who witness the persecution Christians are suffering for their faith?

In what ways does this outcome change your perspective and motivation to serve God faithfully no matter what the cost?

Prayerfully read 2 Timothy 1:8–12:

Therefore do not be ashamed of the testimony about our Lord, nor of me his prisoner, but share in suffering for the gospel by the power of God, who saved us and called us to a holy calling, not because of our works but because of his own purpose and grace, which he gave us in Christ Jesus before the ages began, and which now has been manifested through the appearing of our Savior

Christ Jesus, who abolished death and brought life and immortality to light through the gospel, for which I was appointed a preacher and apostle and teacher, which is why I suffer as I do. But I am not ashamed, for I know whom I have believed, and I am convinced that he is able to guard until that Day what has been entrusted to me.

If you are a follower of Jesus, you have a holy calling. You have been entrusted with a life-giving message to live by and to share with others regardless of how they respond to it. Set aside some time to consider this passage in order to grasp the meaning of every phrase and what it means to your walk with Jesus.

Then write in your own words your testimony as to why you are not ashamed to serve Jesus and what you are so convinced about that you are willing to suffer for the gospel of Christ.

Consider the calling that you share with your persecuted brothers and sisters in Christ and what they endure to live out that calling. As a result of what you have learned, how are you better able to pray earnestly and faithfully for them?

Joy

*Blessed are you when people hate you and when they exclude you
and revile you and spurn your name as evil, on account of the
Son of Man! Rejoice in that day, and leap for joy, for behold, your
reward is great in heaven; for so their fathers did to the prophets.*

Luke 6:22–23

Session Start-Up

When we think of words to describe our persecuted family in Christ,
joy may not be at the top of our list. But it is one of the most amazing
qualities we see in many followers of Jesus who endure persecution.
And their joy shouldn't surprise us. After all, the Bible tells us that
Jesus endured the cross with joy because he knew that his sacrifice
would enable us to live with him forever. Jesus also taught his followers to rejoice when others hated and mistreated them because of their
relationship with him.

Joy is evidence of God's Spirit at work in the life of a Christian.
Certainly our brothers and sisters in the faith would prefer not to
suffer, and we are pained by the hardship and abuse they face. But

having joy while suffering persecution is possible because enduring persecution for the sake of Christ is about so much more than pain and suffering. Rejoicing in persecution is about participating in God's redemptive work on earth and the hope of a glorious eternity with him!

If our joy depends on comfortable and happy life circumstances, we are in serious trouble when persecution comes. The Bible clearly teaches us to focus on a reality that is greater than our circumstances: "If then you have been raised with Christ, seek the things that are above, where Christ is, seated at the right hand of God. Set your mind on things that are above, not on things that are on earth" (Colossians 3:1–2). Focusing on Christ and what lies ahead in eternity fills us with joy that cannot be held back, even when we have no earthly reason to rejoice. Let us join with our persecuted brothers and sisters in Christ as they find life and purpose with God in the midst of desperately difficult circumstances.

Prayer

Dear heavenly Father, it is not easy for us to comprehend the relationship between joy and persecution. These aren't words we naturally put together. And yet we often see joy in our persecuted brothers and sisters even while they endure painful, heartbreaking persecution. So, Lord, open our hearts and minds to comprehend the depth of your love for us and to know the truth of the eternal hope we have in your salvation. Teach us what it means to live in the joy of your salvation no matter what circumstances we face. In Jesus's precious name we pray, amen.

Video Exploration
Video Notes

Convert to Islam or we take your sons

I feel afraid for everything

The words of Jesus are different

The enemy destroys; Jesus brings life

Video Discussion

1. When we consider the ways many persecuted Christians are able to endure their suffering with courage and even joy, we are inclined to view them as superheroes who are somehow immune from the pain of their experience. How does the interview with the woman with two sons help you to realize the very real pain and suffering our persecuted family is experiencing?

In what ways is this woman responding in a manner similar to or different from the way you might respond?

What are your thoughts for her and for your fellow believers who are part of the massive human tragedy playing out in the Middle East?

2. When we realize that many of our persecuted brothers and sisters have dealt with losses as difficult as this woman has experienced, and at one point may have felt just as she did at the time she was

interviewed, what do you think about the fact that they are able to grow into a place of peace, trust, and joy in the Lord?

What do you think must happen for a transformation from despair to joy to take place?

3. It is so shocking to learn of the brutality of the persecution our Christian family faces in Syria and Iraq that we may overlook the bigger picture of all that has been taken from them. They often have lost family members—in some cases all of them. They have lost everything (or nearly everything) they have ever owned. They have no way to provide food, shelter, clothing, medicine, or education for themselves or their families. And there is no hope that they will recoup their losses or ever return to the life they once had. It is not an overstatement to say, "All our dreams are destroyed—everything is destroyed in our life."

When people face circumstances as grave as these, what hope does Jesus offer, and why is that hope so important?

How essential is a relationship with Jesus when we are up against humanly impossible circumstances, and what difference does that relationship make to us?

What does it mean to you when you see your fellow believers face such difficult circumstances with joy and an undiminished desire to serve Jesus faithfully?

What is your persecuted family helping you to realize about living with the expectancy that God is faithful, present, and working for good no matter what our life situation may be?

> We expect Christians living in the hotbed of Iraq
> or Syria to be superhero Christians. But they're not.
> They're just like me. They don't put on a superhero
> cape every day, but God gives them the courage
> to continue to share the gospel. It is incredibly
> encouraging to me that I don't have to be a super-
> hero Christian to share the gospel.
>
> Olive S.

Bible Perspective

It is deeply troubling to consider the depth of the brutality, hatred, and disrespect that ISIS and other Islamic extremists have for the lives of our brothers and sisters in Christ (as well as for others who do not submit to the rule of Islam). The enemy of God and his people clearly is hard at work to cripple and destroy the trust, peace, and joy of our relationship with God. But that enemy has no power over Jesus, our Savior. Jesus has already defeated him. And Jesus has given his followers his Spirit and his Word so that we can know how to walk faithfully with him and experience the joy of our salvation no matter what our circumstances may be.

1. What does Jesus want us to experience in our relationship with him, and how is it possible? "As the Father has loved me, so have

I loved you. Abide in my love. If you keep my commandments, you will abide in my love, just as I have kept my Father's commandments and abide in his love. These things I have spoken to you, that my joy may be in you, and that your joy may be full" (John 15:9–11).

2. From a human perspective, life is about what we acquire, what we enjoy, and the power we have to control our experiences. In contrast, Romans 14:17 tells us what God's perspective is all about: "For the kingdom of God is not a matter of eating and drinking but of righteousness and peace and joy in the Holy Spirit."

> What comfort and encouragement do you think this statement brings to our persecuted brothers and sisters who have lost control of everything that, at least from a human perspective, is valuable in life?

> As you have watched this video series, in what ways have you seen your persecuted family in Christ live out the values of God's kingdom?

3. In his letter of encouragement to the Christians at Colossae, notice that Paul did not pray for their happiness, comfort, or even their physical needs: "And so, from the day we heard, we have not ceased to pray for you, asking that you may be filled with the knowledge of his will in all spiritual wisdom and understanding, so as to walk in a manner worthy of the Lord, fully pleasing to him, bearing fruit in every good work and increasing in the

knowledge of God. May you be strengthened with all power, according to his glorious might, for all endurance and patience with joy" (Colossians 1:9–11).

Instead of material comfort, what did Paul pray for?

Why are the things Paul prayed for important to Christians who are persecuted for their faith?

Think back to the persecuted Christians you have been introduced to in this video series. Which of the things Paul prayed for have they demonstrated as they live out their commitment to Christ?

4. Paul's second letter to the Christians in Corinth gives us a picture of the paradox of suffering for Jesus—facing great pain and difficulty yet having hope and joy in faithfully making him known.

a. Notice the insights 2 Corinthians 4:7–11 provides: "But we have this treasure in jars of clay, to show that the surpassing power belongs to God and not to us. We are afflicted in every way, but not crushed; perplexed, but not driven to despair; persecuted, but not forsaken; struck down, but not destroyed; always carrying in the body the death of Jesus, so that the life of Jesus may also be manifested in our bodies. For we who live are always being given over to death for Jesus's sake, so that the life of Jesus also may be manifested in our mortal flesh."

In what ways do you see our persecuted brothers and sisters in Iraq demonstrating the treasure of faith in Jesus in the manner Paul describes?

What are your thoughts as you consider their faithfulness?

b. Paul continues to emphasize the theme of extreme contrasts in 2 Corinthians 6:8–10: "We are treated as impostors, and yet are true; as unknown, and yet well known; as dying, and behold, we live; as punished, and yet not killed; as sorrowful, yet always rejoicing; as poor, yet making many rich; as having nothing, yet possessing everything."

How well does this describe the circumstances and faithfulness of our persecuted family in Iraq?

What do you realize, from this passage and the example of your persecuted family, about walking faithfully with Jesus through oppressive circumstances?

5. There is no denying that God is at work today in the midst of great turmoil, affliction, and persecution, redeeming those who are lost in sin. In what ways do you see 1 Thessalonians 1:5-6 being lived out by your brothers and sisters in the persecuted church? "Our gospel came to you not only in word, but also in power and in the Holy Spirit and with full conviction. You know what kind of men we proved to be among you for your sake. And you became imitators of us and of the Lord, for you received the word in much affliction, with the joy of the Holy Spirit."

This war is like a knife in the heart of the church. No human can stand that suffering. But there is God's presence. I can see Christ in the midst of the darkness.

A VOM contact, Syria

Our Response

Joy in the Lord is a life-giving gift and a powerful weapon in the hands of believers who are willing to endure persecution and give up everything in order to love, serve, and obey Jesus, our Savior. Confidence in God's abiding presence with us, trust that he is accomplishing his work through us, and belief that we will spend eternity with him change our perspective from despair to hope. Living in the joy of our Lord defeats the enemy who comes to kill, steal, and destroy.

Everywhere he went to share the gospel, the apostle Paul was persecuted—beaten, imprisoned, and finally killed. As long as he had breath to keep going, he endured it all. But even more amazing than his endurance is the joy he had even when he suffered greatly. In 2 Corinthians 7:4–6 he wrote, "In all our affliction, I am overflowing with joy ... Our bodies had no rest ... we were afflicted at every turn—fighting without and fear within."

In the same spirit of faithful obedience and joy, Peter and other apostles kept teaching the good news of Jesus even when the authorities had forbidden them to do so. What was their response to being jailed and beaten? When they were released, they left, "rejoicing that they were counted worthy to suffer dishonor for the name [Jesus]" (Acts 5:41).

In what ways are our persecuted brothers and sisters continuing to demonstrate the apostles' example of faithfulness with joy?

How does their example help you to see joy in response to persecution in new ways?

Everyone who follows Jesus is a partner with those who suffer for his sake. Hebrews 10:32–34 reminds us of this unity with our persecuted family: "But recall the former days when, after you were enlightened, you endured a hard struggle with sufferings, sometimes being publicly exposed to reproach and affliction, and sometimes being partners with those so treated. For you had compassion on those in prison, and you joyfully accepted the plundering of your property, since you knew that you yourselves had a better possession and an abiding one."

What impact have the believers you have been introduced to thus far in this study had on you? On how you view your circumstances? On how you view and experience joy in your relationship with Jesus?

We have the privilege of expressing compassion for our brothers and sisters who face the reproach and affliction of persecution. What are some of the ways you would be willing to be a partner with your persecuted family?

The prophet Habakkuk knew that desperate times were ahead. God's people would have to endure difficult, frightening, and painful circumstances. "Though the fig tree should not blossom, nor fruit be on the vines, the produce of the olive fail and the fields yield no food, the flock be cut off from the fold and there be no herd in the stalls, yet I will rejoice in the LORD; I will take joy in the God of my salvation" (Habakkuk 3:17–18).

What crucial choice did Habakkuk make regarding what lay ahead?

Why is that an important choice for believers to make today, particularly when we face persecution?

Closing Prayer

Let us join our hearts together before God and pray for the body of Christ. Let us begin our prayer together, then continue with individual prayers as each of us is led, until we close.

Dear Lord, we come before you in need—in need of your presence, your strength, and your joy. May we be faithful to stand for you so that nothing can rob us of the joy that overcomes the enemy who comes to kill, steal, and destroy. We pray for … [prayers of the group] … Thank you for the privilege of standing with our persecuted family in Christ as they risk everything to bring honor to your name and share the good news of Jesus through word and action. May we always be faithful. In Jesus's name we pray, amen.

Next Steps
Restoring Our Joy in the Lord

All of us face times when hardship or sorrow overwhelms us, when evil threatens to destroy our joy. During such times, God's Word is a powerful tool for keeping us focused on what is true, unchangeable, and life-giving. When the difficulties we face leave us discouraged and disheartened, God's Word reminds us of what is true and can help to restore our joy.

For a fresh reminder of where our joy comes from and what enables us to rejoice in all circumstances, read and meditate on the following passages of Scripture. Pray them for yourself, for your loved ones when you know they are struggling, and for your persecuted family in Jesus whose joy the enemy is seeking to steal.

> Beloved, do not be surprised at the fiery trial when it comes upon you to test you, as though something strange were happening to you. But rejoice insofar as you share Christ's sufferings, that you may also rejoice and be glad when his glory is revealed. (1 Peter 4:12–13)

> I have set the LORD always before me;
>> because he is at my right hand, I shall not be
>> shaken.

> Therefore my heart is glad, and my whole being
>> rejoices;
>> my flesh also dwells secure.
> For you will not abandon my soul to Sheol,
>> or let your holy one see corruption.

You make known to me the path of life;
in your presence there is fullness of joy;
at your right hand are pleasures forevermore.
(Psalm 16:8–11)

But let all who take refuge in you rejoice;
let them ever sing for joy,
and spread your protection over them,
that those who love your name may exult in you.
(Psalm 5:11)

Therefore, since we have been justified by faith, we have peace with God through our Lord Jesus Christ. Through him we have also obtained access by faith into this grace in which we stand, and we rejoice in hope of the glory of God. (Romans 5:1–2)

Many are the sorrows of the wicked,
but steadfast love surrounds the one who
trusts in the LORD.
Be glad in the LORD, and rejoice, O righteous,
and shout for joy, all you upright in heart!
(Psalm 32:10–11)

May the God of hope fill you with all joy and peace in believing, so that by the power of the Holy Spirit you may abound in hope. (Romans 15:13)

Perseverance

And you will be hated by all for my name's sake. But
the one who endures to the end will be saved.

Mark 13:13

Session Start-Up

Every day in communities in Iraq and other countries where Islamic extremists exert control, followers of Jesus pay a high price for persevering in their faith. They endure fierce hostility, great hardship, brutal attacks, and unimaginable losses because they refuse to deny Jesus. They stand firm in their commitment to their Lord and Savior and, in the midst of overwhelming opposition, steadfastly fulfill his purpose for their lives.

To persevere, or endure, for the cause of Jesus Christ means to stand firm and resist whatever opposition rises against us. The picture that comes to mind is that of a person who plants his feet and leans into a strong wind or pushes back against a powerful river current. It's not something we can do well in our own strength.

Jesus knew what his followers would face in the future, so he taught his disciples how necessary it was to maintain a life-giving relationship with him. He said, "As the branch cannot bear fruit by itself, unless it abides in the vine, neither can you, unless you abide in me. I am the vine; you are the branches ... apart from me you can do nothing" (John 15:4–5).

If our desire is to be followers of Jesus who stand up and serve him faithfully, we, too, must abide in him. We must be grounded in the Word and character of God. We must cling to our relationship with Jesus, growing ever closer to him as we learn to walk with him by faith.

The persecuted Christians we meet today will challenge us to join them in standing firmly for God and obediently fulfilling his purpose for our lives—no matter what the cost. The strength of their relationship with their Lord and Savior empowers them to persevere—to "run with endurance the race" that is set before them (Hebrews 12:1). Let's pay close attention to these faithful believers whose example of faith and strength of relationship with their Lord and Savior can deeply touch our lives.

Prayer

Dear Lord, we come before you seeking to become better acquainted with our persecuted family and to learn to walk in your ways. Guide us as we watch the video, delve into your Word, and learn how you want us to respond. Thank you that you are faithful to provide everything we need for life and the strength to persevere in serving you. We are grateful for this opportunity to gather together without the threat of being arrested, tortured, or killed as many of our family in faith are. In the name of Jesus we pray, amen.

Video Exploration
Video Notes

Ordinary people under attack
Struggling to live with the unknown
The life-changing presence of Jesus
Empowered to endure to the end

Video Discussion

1. Some of the Christians we have been introduced to in this video series are pastors, but others are ordinary people who went about life going to work, caring for their families, or attending school when severe persecution suddenly changed everything in their lives.

How "prepared" do you think they were for what happened to them, and what does their experience lead you to think about concerning the strength of your commitment to Christ and what it takes to be faithful to him when you encounter persecution?

These Christians are not new to persecution and suffering. They have been facing it for quite some time, and there is no reason to expect it will end soon. How does the fact that they are facing a long-term crisis, not just a temporary setback, impact your understanding of them, their commitment to Jesus, and their material and spiritual needs?

2. What struggles have you faced during times of upheaval and uncertainty in your life, and what do you think would be your greatest struggles if you were to experience the uncertainty of not knowing if your loved ones are dead or alive? Or if people who want to harm you will find you? Or if your need for food and shelter to survive will be met?

How could you persevere under the kinds of threats and uncertainty of the circumstances our family in Christ faces?

What have your persecuted brothers and sisters helped you to understand about what it means to depend on God in order to persevere for one more hour, one more day, etc.?

3. Our persecuted family is persevering not only in the sense of surviving difficult circumstances moment by moment, they also are persevering spiritually. What do you notice about the way they are growing in their relationship and commitment to Jesus?

4. Two of the people interviewed in this video had done the best they could to persevere but reached a point where they could do no more—Safwan because he was nearly dead, and Ban because she tried to kill herself.

What did people who recognized their desperate condition do for them, and what did God do for them?

How did God's intervention change them?

What does this lead you to think about the importance of reaching out to help our persecuted family?

Iraqi Christians Persevere

Since 2003, more than two-thirds of the 1.5 million Christians who lived in Iraq have fled, emigrated, or been killed. Many families have lost loved ones. Some families have known when their loved ones died and were able to bury them. Other families have no idea if their loved ones are dead; they have simply disappeared. These losses are very difficult to bear, yet our fellow Christians persevere.

The father, brothers, and sister of Inaam Isho Poulos, for example, lived in Qaraqosh. They now camp out in an empty office in Erbil. They know what happened to their beloved daughter and sister. On the day she was to be engaged, an ISIS mortar killed the thirty-six-year-old woman and two neighborhood children.

Inaam's family recognizes that her tragic death was not in vain. The mortar attack initiated an exodus from the city that her sister says "began just in time. Thousands of people were rescued by her death." Many women who might otherwise have been taken by ISIS were able to escape.

Following the mortar attack, the church bells on the Plain of Nineveh rang out to warn the people. After that night, when the Christians fled, the church bells stopped ringing. For the first time in sixteen hundred years, they fell silent.

But our Christian brothers and sisters in Iraq have not given up. Abuna Mazen Ishoa, who formerly pastored a church in Qaraqosh, does not know if he will ever be able to return to that city. Even before the ISIS takeover of northern Iraq, Islamic extremists had kidnapped and held him captive for a week. They also had slaughtered his father and brothers in their own home.

In spite of the opposition, Abuna believes that God is at work and will make a way for his people. For now, Abuna provides spiritual support for displaced Christians camped in Erbil and hopes in the future to manage a monastery in Iraq. "Yes," he says, "here in Iraq! Christianity will remain here!" (adapted from SDOK).

Bible Perspective

In the Muslim world, our family in Christ has been persevering for a long time. In some areas the persecution is primarily social or economic in nature—denying justice or employment and exclusion from housing or educational opportunities. In other areas, Islamic extremists have had free reign to attack, kidnap, or kill Christians as they wish. So the example our brothers and sisters in Christ provide of what it means to persevere while enduring persecution is extraordinary.

Even more amazing is their commitment to engage on the spiritual battlefield. They are not glumly sitting on the sidelines, just barely hanging on until their circumstances improve. Quite the opposite: they are intent not only to walk with God but also to serve him and eagerly share the gospel message with people who live in spiritual darkness. Let's see what insight the Bible provides about what motivates and enables followers of Jesus to persevere with unstoppable zeal for the Lord.

1. Jesus was persecuted and eventually killed for proclaiming his life-giving message to the world in which he lived. On one occasion he said, "I am the way, and the truth, and the life" (John 14:6). On another he said, "Truly, truly, I say to you, whoever hears my word and believes him who sent me has eternal life. He does not come into judgment, but has passed from death to life" (John 5:24).

To what extent do you think we view telling others about the message of Jesus as literally bringing words of life to them?

How does our perspective affect our commitment and eagerness in sharing the gospel?

2. One example of how the apostles endured persecution and eagerly continued to teach as God had instructed them is found in Acts 5:17–21: "But the high priest rose up, and all who were with him (that is, the party of the Sadducees), and filled with jealousy they arrested the apostles and put them in the public prison. But during the night an angel of the Lord opened the prison doors and brought them out, and said, 'Go and stand in the temple and speak to the people all the words of this Life.' And

when they heard this, they entered the temple at daybreak and began to teach."

What conviction was far greater in the hearts and minds of the apostles than the threat of persecution?

How important does this conviction seem to be in the hearts and minds of our Christian brothers and sisters who minister among those who have been displaced by the advance of Islamic extremists?

3. It is not easy to persevere and be spiritually fruitful when we face the uncertainty and daily struggles of life as a persecuted Christian. Yet some of our fellow believers seem to be undeterred by the chaos. What does Jesus say is necessary for us, his followers, to be spiritually fruitful in our walk with God, no matter what our circumstances may be? "Abide in me, and I in you. As the branch cannot bear fruit by itself, unless it abides in the vine, neither can you, unless you abide in me. I am the vine; you are the branches. Whoever abides in me and I in him, he it is that bears much fruit, for apart from me you can do nothing" (John 15:4–5).

4. When writing letters of instruction and encouragement to the early churches, the apostle Paul used the language of athletic competition to describe the mind-set needed to persevere spiritually. Let's consider how his instructions can keep us on track to fulfill God's purpose for us.

a. "Let us run with endurance the race that is set before us, looking to Jesus, the founder and perfecter of our faith, who for the joy that was set before him endured the cross, despising the shame, and is seated at the right hand of the throne of God" (Hebrews 12:1–2).

Where does our focus need to be if we are to "run" well, and why?

b. "Do you not know that in a race all the runners run, but only one receives the prize? So run that you may obtain it. Every athlete exercises self-control in all things. They do it to receive a perishable wreath, but we an imperishable. So I do not run aimlessly; I do not box as one beating the air. But I discipline my body and keep it under control, lest after preaching to others I myself should be disqualified" (1 Corinthians 9:24–27).

Which spiritual disciplines do you think are necessary for maintaining self-control so that we do not run aimlessly?

c. "But one thing I do: forgetting what lies behind and straining forward to what lies ahead, I press on toward the goal for the prize of the upward call of God in Christ Jesus" (Philippians 3:13–14).

How hard are we willing to work in order to persevere to the end?

5. What assurance do we have that faithfulness in sharing Jesus's words of life with those who do not know him matters, and why is that assurance important to us? "Therefore … be steadfast, immovable, always abounding in the work of the Lord, knowing that in the Lord your labor is not in vain" (1 Corinthians 15:58).

6. There is no question that the apostle Paul was persecuted relentlessly and through it all remained a faithful servant of the Lord. In his closing letter to Timothy, his colaborer in ministry, Paul writes, "For I am already being poured out as a drink offering, and the time of my departure has come. I have fought the good fight, I have finished the race, I have kept the faith. Henceforth there is laid up for me the crown of righteousness, which the Lord, the righteous judge, will award to me on that Day, and not only to me but also to all who have loved his appearing" (2 Timothy 4:6–8).

What example has our persecuted family in Iraq given us of this kind of spiritual perseverance?

In what ways does their example urge us to persevere faithfully?

Christians are the root of Iraq. We need to share the love of Jesus to everyone. If there is a place without the love of Jesus, it will be a very dark place and no peace or hope will exist there.

Lina, Iraq

Our Response

The aggressive rise of ISIS since 2014 certainly has escalated the persecution of our Christian brothers and sisters in Syria and Iraq to a massive and unprecedented scale. There is no reason to expect a swift end to their suffering, but there is great hope and encouragement to be found in the way they persevere in their suffering. Because these believers are our family and our partners in ministry, we must ask ourselves what our role might be in supporting them and serving with them. Acts 11:19–23 describes a situation not unlike what is happening in Iraq and Syria today:

> Now those who were scattered because of the persecution that arose over Stephen traveled as far as Phoenicia and Cyprus and Antioch, speaking the word to no one except Jews. But there were some of them, men of Cyprus and Cyrene, who on coming to Antioch spoke to the Hellenists also, preaching the Lord Jesus. And the hand of the Lord was with them, and a great number who believed turned to the Lord. The report of this came to the ears of the church in Jerusalem, and they sent Barnabas to Antioch. When he came and saw the grace of God, he was glad, and he exhorted them all to remain faithful to the Lord with steadfast purpose.

In what ways was the situation the early Christians faced similar to what is happening among the Christian refugees who are being scattered by the advance of ISIS?

As was true during the days of the early church, many of those who are being persecuted are undaunted in their mission to faithfully proclaim the gospel of Christ. Who are persecuted believers reaching with the gospel today?

What is your response to their faithfulness in proclaiming the gospel, and how will you express it to your persecuted family and to God?

The apostle Paul was willing to pay any personal cost in order to obey Christ by sharing the gospel, and he knew that God would supply strength to endure. Yet in Philippians 4:11–14, we see how much the support of his family in Christ meant to him: "Not that I am speaking of being in need, for I have learned in whatever situation I am to be content. I know how to be brought low, and I know how to abound. In any and every circumstance, I have learned the secret of facing plenty and hunger, abundance and need. I can do all things through him who strengthens me. Yet it was kind of you to share my trouble."

What do you think it means to our persecuted brothers and sisters to know that they are remembered by their Christian family around the world?

In what ways are you willing to share in the troubles of your family in Christ and express the kindheartedness of God by supporting and serving them?

We can always pray for the physical needs—protection and provision—of our persecuted family in Christ, but sometimes it can be hard to know how to pray for their spiritual needs—for their faith and ministry. Colossians 1:9–14 helps to inform a supportive response to the needs of our brothers and sisters as they endure persecution:

> And so, from the day we heard, we have not ceased to pray for you, asking that you may be filled with the knowledge of his will in all spiritual wisdom and understanding, so as to walk in a manner worthy of the Lord, fully pleasing to him, bearing fruit in every good work and increasing in the knowledge of God. May you be strengthened with all power, according to his glorious might, for all endurance and patience with joy, giving thanks to the Father, who has qualified you to share in the inheritance of the saints in light. He has delivered us from the domain of darkness and transferred us to the kingdom of his beloved Son, in whom we have redemption, the forgiveness of sins.

In accordance with this passage, what specific needs can we pray for on behalf of our persecuted brothers and sisters in Iraq?

From what you have seen of their needs and sincere desire to serve the Lord, what difference might your prayers make in their lives and ministry?

How eager are you to participate with them in prayer as they serve God, and how else might you support them and share in the work God is accomplishing through them?

Closing Prayer

Let us close our time together in prayer.

Thank you, Lord Jesus, that our Christian brothers and sisters who are suffering persecution chose you above all else. We thank you that as hard, painful, and uncertain as their circumstances are that they are willing to give up everything to proclaim you as their Savior and Lord. Bless them with your presence and provision in the midst of the storm. Protect them from those who want to silence them. Open our hearts to learn how we can stand with them, support them, and encourage them. And, Lord, whatever persecution may lie ahead for us, may we be faithful to choose you and endure to the end. In your precious name we pray, amen.

Next Steps
The Practices and Attitudes of Perseverance

It is impossible to sacrifice and persevere through persecution as courageous, faithful, joyful, forgiving servants of Christ if we try to do it in our own strength. The only way to survive the hardship *and* to be fruitful in fulfilling God's purpose for our lives is to be engaged in a life-giving relationship with Jesus. To have such a relationship, we must be intimately rooted in what the Bible reveals about his character and teachings.

In a sense, the entire Bible teaches us how to persevere in faith for the long haul. It helps us to know the character of God and to draw near him. It provides trustworthy guidance on how to live in obedience. It teaches us what brings honor to his name. It trains us to discern what is of God and, therefore, valuable and what is not. It gives us hope for the future. As you read the following Bible passages, consider not only the ways in which our persecuted family in Christ lives out these practices and attitudes but how we can grow in these qualities in order to live faithfully for Jesus as well.

The disciple Peter was a passionate follower of Jesus. He learned the hard way what being faithful to Jesus under the threat of persecution demands. (Remember, Peter denied Jesus on the night he was betrayed.) In 2 Peter 1:5–10 he writes:

> For this very reason, make every effort to supplement your faith with virtue, and virtue with knowledge, and knowledge with self-control, and

self-control with steadfastness, and steadfastness with godliness, and godliness with brotherly affection, and brotherly affection with love. For if these qualities are yours and are increasing, they keep you from being ineffective or unfruitful in the knowledge of our Lord Jesus Christ. For whoever lacks these qualities is so nearsighted that he is blind, having forgotten that he was cleansed from his former sins. Therefore, brothers, be all the more diligent to confirm your calling and election, for if you practice these qualities you will never fall.

If we develop the qualities Peter describes, what will be the result?

How much do you want the promise of a fruitful life in Jesus to be fulfilled in you, and what steps will you take to pursue it?

One of the amazing qualities we see in many of our persecuted brothers and sisters in Christ is their passion and joy as they seek to fulfill God's calling and bring the news of salvation to people who need it. What kind of people does Titus tell us God needs to accomplish his work, and how do we become like that? "For the grace of God has appeared, bringing salvation for all people, training us to renounce ungodliness and worldly passions, and to live self-controlled, upright, and godly lives in the present age, waiting for our blessed hope, the appearing of the glory of our great God and Savior Jesus Christ, who gave himself for us to redeem us from

all lawlessness and to purify for himself a people for his own possession who are zealous for good works" (Titus 2:11–14).

We are all born into sin, and not one of us naturally has what
God calls a "pure heart." Yet God redeems our hearts and makes
us fit to serve him. If we want to persevere, however, we must
pursue his righteousness: "So flee youthful passions and pursue
righteousness, faith, love, and peace, along with those who call on
the Lord from a pure heart" (2 Timothy 2:22).

As you read the following passages, consider the work God
wants to accomplish in your heart and life. Write down for
yourself the things you must pursue and the things you must
"put away" in order to persevere and be a fruitful witness for the
gospel. Consider also the ministry of your persecuted family in
Christ and how quickly the gospel message could be silenced if
they are not faithful to obey him wholeheartedly.

> Beloved, I urge you as sojourners and exiles to
> abstain from the passions of the flesh, which
> wage war against your soul. (1 Peter 2:11)

> Put off your old self, which belongs to your
> former manner of life and is corrupt through
> deceitful desires, and to be renewed in the spirit
> of your minds, and to put on the new self, created
> after the likeness of God in true righteousness
> and holiness. (Ephesians 4:22–24)

Put to death therefore what is earthly in you: sexual immorality, impurity, passion, evil desire, and covetousness, which is idolatry. On account of these the wrath of God is coming. In these you too once walked, when you were living in them. But now you must put them all away: anger, wrath, malice, slander, and obscene talk from your mouth. Do not lie to one another, seeing that you have put off the old self with its practices and have put on the new self, which is being renewed in knowledge after the image of its creator. (Colossians 3:5–10)

Do not be conformed to this world, but be transformed by the renewal of your mind, that by testing you may discern what is the will of God, what is good and acceptable and perfect. (Romans 12:2)

It is important to remember that we do not persevere alone. Each of us perseveres for one Lord, for one calling, and together we persevere to share the good news of the kingdom of God. For that reason, how we persevere, serve, and minister, and the way we treat one another, has an impact on other members of our family in Christ. Paul, in Colossians 3:14–17, admonishes us to "put on love, which binds everything together in perfect harmony. And let the peace of Christ rule in your hearts, to which indeed you were called in one body. And be thankful. Let the word of Christ dwell in you richly, teaching and admonishing one another in all wisdom, singing psalms and hymns and spiritual songs, with thankfulness in your hearts to God. And whatever you do, in word or deed, do everything in the name of the Lord Jesus, giving thanks to God the Father through him."

What difference can it make when believers express love for one another in the body of Christ, especially for our members who are enduring persecution, and how have you seen this demonstrated in the video series?

What is your desire and commitment to "put on love" and encourage your persecuted family in Jesus?

Above all else, 1 Chronicles 16:11 tells us to "seek the LORD and his strength; seek his presence continually!"

Session 5

Forgiveness

*Bearing with one another and, if one has a complaint
against another, forgiving each other; as the Lord
has forgiven you, so you also must forgive.*

Colossians 3:13

Session Start-Up

The trauma and violence our brothers and sisters in Christ suffer because of their faith in Jesus prompts many powerful responses. We reel from the grief and pain of it. We react to the injustice with outrage and anger. We entertain thoughts of retaliation and revenge. And God understands these responses. His heart is grieved too. His righteous anger burns. As sovereign Lord of the universe, he holds those who do evil accountable.

But above all else, God loves. He loves his persecuted children, and he loves those who persecute them. God's heart of love longs for everyone who despises followers of Jesus to turn away from evil and accept his gift of forgiveness and eternal life.

How will those who persecute Christians discover God's love for them? They discover it as the very people they persecute extend God's sincere love and forgiveness toward them! It is not an easy thing for a suffering Christian to turn around and love the person who has caused such pain. In fact, such forgiveness is humanly abnormal. Without God's intervention in our hearts and minds, it is impossible.

Jesus has commanded all who follow him to love our enemies and bless people who abuse us. As our persecuted brothers and sisters in Christ choose to obey this command and grow in their relationship with God, he accomplishes a miracle in their hearts. They begin to see their abusers through God's eyes. They grow into a desire to forgive with the love and compassion Jesus expressed as he died on the cross, praying, "Father, forgive them, for they know not what they do" (Luke 23:34).

The persecuted Christians we will meet in this video express amazing love toward those who have oppressed and abused them. No matter how much they have suffered, they have chosen to forgive their persecutors rather than hate them because they know that this is what God desires. They sincerely want Muslims to know that God will forgive their sins. They want to share God's gift of eternal life with them. What can we learn about God's love and forgiveness from our persecuted family in Jesus?

Prayer

Dear Lord, forgiveness isn't easy for us. Too often we respond in anger or retaliate rather than allowing you to heal our wounded hearts and grow an attitude of love and forgiveness within us. We are guilty of accepting forgiveness from you yet withholding forgiveness from those who have wronged us. We ask you to teach us to walk in your love and to forgive others as you have forgiven us. May our hearts be open to what you want us to learn as we see how our persecuted family in Christ walks your path of forgiveness. In Jesus's name we pray, amen.

Video Exploration
Video Notes

Persecuted for their faith in Christ

Born into a religion

A death pact becomes a miracle

Discovering the God of love

Forgive them, for they do not know what they do

Video Discussion

1. As Westerners, we don't readily understand the essential role religion plays in Middle Eastern culture and in a person's identity. Nor do we understand how permanent one's religious affiliation is. In what ways did the video help you to better understand the intense turmoil that Islamic extremism is creating in Muslim culture today—both for those who are intent on destroying any perceived threat to their religion and for those who are shocked to discover that Islam is not what they thought it was?

2. When Padina described how hard she had tried to adhere to the rules of Islam exactly, yet felt empty, desperate, and distant from Allah, what were your thoughts and feelings for her?

What did her story help you to realize about Islam that you didn't know before?

What insight did you gain into how difficult it is for a Muslim to even consider accepting another religion?

3. From a human perspective, it is easy to respond to the violence and killing committed in the name of Allah with rage and revenge. Yet this is not what we have seen in the hearts of persecuted Christians interviewed in this video series.

What surprised you about how much your persecuted family wants their persecutors to discover Jesus, receive forgiveness for their sins, and obtain the promise of eternal life?

What motivates and enables our persecuted brothers and sisters to love and forgive those who have persecuted them?

4. What impact does the love these Christians express for their Muslim persecutors—their genuine desire to forgive, their understanding that those who harm them don't know what they are doing, their longing for Muslims to have eternal life—have on you?

Do you think you could respond as they do if placed in similar situations? Why or why not?

Bible Perspective

Love. Compassion. Kindness. Peace. Forgiveness. We often do not use these words to describe our feelings toward those who hate and persecute us because of our faith in Jesus. Yet over and over again these words accurately express what our persecuted brothers and sisters in Iraq feel toward their persecutors. What makes such love and forgiveness possible? It begins with an understanding of what the Bible reveals about God's perspective on forgiving those who persecute us.

1. Forgiveness is an act of love, and it is not a natural human response to persecution. Forgiveness is, however, thoroughly rooted in the love and character of God. Consider the following brief descriptions of God's forgiveness:

> For you, O Lord, are good and forgiving,
>> abounding in steadfast love to all who call
>>> upon you. (Psalm 86:5)

> But you are a God ready to forgive, gracious and merciful, slow to anger and abounding in steadfast love. (Nehemiah 9:17)

> If we confess our sins, he is faithful and just to forgive us our sins and to cleanse us from all unrighteousness. (1 John 1:9)

Based on these descriptions of God's character, who would he exclude from receiving his forgiveness?

Which qualities of his love and forgiveness do you think God wants those who follow him to emulate?

2. In Isaiah's prophetic psalm about Jesus, he portrays a man who is persecuted and afflicted so that others could be forgiven. As we read Isaiah 53:3–10, 12, think about not only what Jesus suffered on our behalf, but the example of love, compassion, self-sacrifice, and forgiveness he provides for us to follow as we walk with him.

> He was despised and rejected by men;
> a man of sorrows, and acquainted with
> grief;
> and as one from whom men hide their faces
> he was despised, and we esteemed him not.

> Surely he has borne our griefs
> and carried our sorrows;
> yet we esteemed him stricken,
> smitten by God, and afflicted.
> But he was pierced for our transgressions;
> he was crushed for our iniquities;
> upon him was the chastisement that brought us
> peace,
> and with his wounds we are healed.
> All we like sheep have gone astray;

we have turned—every one—to his own
    way;
and the LORD has laid on him
    the iniquity of us all.

He was oppressed, and he was afflicted,
    yet he opened not his mouth;
like a lamb that is led to the slaughter,
    and like a sheep that before its shearers is
        silent,
    so he opened not his mouth.
By oppression and judgment he was taken away;
    and as for his generation, who considered
that he was cut off out of the land of the living,
    stricken for the transgression of my people?
And they made his grave with the wicked
    and with a rich man in his death,
although he had done no violence,
    and there was no deceit in his mouth.

Yet it was the will of the LORD to crush him;
    he has put him to grief;
when his soul makes an offering for guilt,

... because he poured out his soul to death
    and was numbered with the transgressors;
yet he bore the sin of many,
    and makes intercession for the transgressors.

In response to all that he suffered, even death on the cross, Jesus said, "Father, forgive them, for they know not what they do" (Luke 23:34).

What does it mean to you that Jesus was willing to suffer all of this so that you could be forgiven?

In what ways does the suffering our persecuted brothers and sisters endure today echo the suffering that Jesus endured on our behalf? Point out some specific examples.

What impact do you think the suffering that persecuted Christians share with Jesus has on their relationship with him?

How willing are we, as Christians, to show the love and forgiveness of Jesus to our persecutors by extending to them the forgiveness that we have received from Jesus?

3. If we want those who view us as their enemies to believe that we love and forgive them, our behavior toward them must be directed by God's Spirit, not by our human emotions. In Luke 6:27–36, Jesus taught us how to respond to people who consider followers of Jesus to be their enemies:

> But I say to you who hear, Love your enemies,
> do good to those who hate you, bless those who
> curse you, pray for those who abuse you. To one
> who strikes you on the cheek, offer the other also,

and from one who takes away your cloak do not withhold your tunic either. Give to everyone who begs from you, and from one who takes away your goods do not demand them back. And as you wish that others would do to you, do so to them.

If you love those who love you, what benefit is that to you? For even sinners love those who love them. And if you do good to those who do good to you, what benefit is that to you? For even sinners do the same. And if you lend to those from whom you expect to receive, what credit is that to you? Even sinners lend to sinners, to get back the same amount. But love your enemies, and do good, and lend, expecting nothing in return, and your reward will be great, and you will be sons of the Most High, for he is kind to the ungrateful and the evil. Be merciful, even as your Father is merciful.

a. Which specific attitudes and behaviors does Jesus want us to have toward those who treat us as their enemies?

List them and discuss the impact that you think such attitudes and behaviors may have on people who hate us because we follow Jesus.

In what ways have we seen these attitudes and behaviors demonstrated by our persecuted brothers and sisters in Iraq?

In what ways might we demonstrate these attitudes and behaviors toward people who hate what we stand for in our communities?

b. Why is it important that we love our enemies and show mercy (who are we representing)?

4. God's desire for us to forgive others is not just a good idea. It is not just a suggestion. In Mark 11:25 Jesus says, "And whenever you stand praying, forgive, if you have anything against anyone, so that your Father also who is in heaven may forgive you your trespasses." And in Matthew 6:12–15 he says, "Forgive us our debts, as we also have forgiven our debtors. And lead us not into temptation, but deliver us from evil. For if you forgive others their trespasses, your heavenly Father will also forgive you, but if you do not forgive others their trespasses, neither will your Father forgive your trespasses."

What impact does Jesus's command to forgive have on our spiritual health and growth?

What changes might we need to make in how we live out our faith in order to put forgiveness in its rightful place?

5. Colossians 3:12–13 presents the qualities and actions that should characterize our interaction with others so that we accurately reflect our identity as God's people: "Put on then, as God's chosen ones, holy and beloved, compassionate hearts, kindness, humility, meekness, and patience, bearing with one another and, if one has a complaint

against another, forgiving each other; as the Lord has forgiven you, so you also must forgive."

What impact can such attitudes and behaviors have on people, even on those who despise us?

Why do you think it is important for us, as followers of Jesus, to conduct our relationships as the Bible describes, especially when we face people who oppose our faith?

It was in prison that we found the hope of salvation for the Communists. It was there that we developed a sense of responsibility toward them. It was in being tortured by them that we learned to love them.

Richard Wurmbrand, founder of
The Voice of the Martyrs

Our Response

Throughout this study series, we have seen how important it is to pray for our persecuted brothers and sisters in Christ. They need our prayers for protection, provision, courage, faithfulness, encouragement, and a strong sense of fellowship with God. Without diminishing our responsibility to support and pray for our persecuted family, we must realize that another group of people needs our prayers as well.

In Matthew 5:43–45, Jesus tells us who they are: "You have heard that it was said, 'You shall love your neighbor and hate your enemy.' But I say to you, Love your enemies and pray for those who persecute you, so that you may be sons of your Father who is in heaven." Pray for those who persecute us? Pray for those who persecute our family in Christ? Yes! They need God's love, forgiveness, and presence too.

How do we pray for those who persecute God's family? The concerns expressed by our persecuted brothers and sisters in Christ give us a starting point:

> They need to realize what they are doing.
> They need God.
> They need Bibles.
> They need followers of Jesus to show them God's love.

What commitment are we willing to make to stand with our persecuted family and earnestly pray for God to meet these needs of their persecutors?

We are rightly concerned about how persecution affects our family in Christ. But 2 Timothy 3:10–13 also describes what happens to those who persecute followers of Jesus: "You, however, have followed my teaching, my conduct, my aim in life, my faith, my patience, my love, my steadfastness, my persecutions and sufferings that happened to me at Antioch, at Iconium, and at Lystra—which persecutions I endured; yet from them all the Lord rescued me. Indeed, all who desire to live a godly life in Christ Jesus will be persecuted, while evil people and impostors will go on from bad to worse, deceiving and being deceived."

If we believe that going from bad to worse is the destiny of people who do evil and do not follow Jesus, how diligently are we willing to pray and work for their salvation?

What might happen if we, as Jesus followers in the West, were to join with our persecuted family in diligently praying for those who persecute Christians—that they will discover God's love for them, that they will realize they desperately need his forgiveness, and that they will find new life in him?

Are we willing to find out? What if we organized a prayer vigil for the persecutors of God's family around the world? What if we designated a regular time to come together and pray for the salvation of those who persecute our family in Christ? What will we do?

Closing Prayer

Let's spend the rest of our time together praying that those who persecute Christians will respond to God's love and seek his forgiveness for their sins, and that our persecuted family will be faithful and fruitful in their efforts to share the love of Christ with those who persecute them.

Dear Lord, you are the God whose love knows no measure, whose forgiveness delivers all of us from bondage to sin and evil. We come together to pray for all who persecute those who follow Jesus ...

[Prayers of the group] … We thank you that we can partner with our persecuted family in praying for their persecutors to find forgiveness and eternal life in you. In the precious name of Jesus we pray, amen.

How to Pray for Our Persecuted Family

Pray that persecuted believers will sense God's presence (Hebrews 13:5).

Pray that they will feel connected to the greater body of Christ (1 Corinthians 12:20, 26).

Pray that they will be comforted by God when their family members are killed, injured, or imprisoned for their witness (2 Corinthians 1:3–5).

Pray that they will have more opportunities to share the gospel (Colossians 4:3).

Pray for their boldness to make Christ known (Philippians 1:14).

Pray that they will forgive and love their persecutors (Matthew 5:44).

Pray that their ministry activities will remain undetected by authorities or others who wish to silence them (Acts 9:20–25).

Pray that they will rejoice in suffering (Acts 5:41).

Pray that they will be refreshed through God's Word and grow in their faith (Ephesians 6:17).

Pray that they will be strengthened through the prayers of fellow believers (Jude verses 20–25).

Next Steps
Who Must I Forgive?

When it comes to persecution or other wrongdoing that is committed against us, we tend to be one-sided in our perspective. We tend to think that what is happening to us is only bad, but God has a different perspective. No matter how painful or difficult our circumstances may be, God is still at work accomplishing his good plan of redemption—even through the bad things that happen to those who follow him faithfully.

Joseph, who saved Israel from a great famine, understood this. When he was a teenager, his older brothers, who hated him, sold him into slavery. For decades, Joseph was faithful to God through many trials—false accusations, imprisonment—and eventually leadership in Pharaoh's kingdom. As God's servant in Pharaoh's domain, Joseph was responsible for storing and distributing food to Egypt and neighboring areas during years of severe famine. While fulfilling these responsibilities, he again encountered his brothers. Notice his forgiveness and focus on the bigger picture of what God sought to accomplish through their wrongdoing:

> So Joseph said to his brothers, "Come near to me, please." And they came near. And he said, "I am your brother, Joseph, whom you sold into Egypt. And now do not be distressed or angry with

yourselves because you sold me here, for God sent me before you to preserve life. For the famine has been in the land these two years, and there are yet five years in which there will be neither plowing nor harvest. And God sent me before you to preserve for you a remnant on earth, and to keep alive for you many survivors. So it was not you who sent me here, but God. (Genesis 45:4–8)

Throughout this video series, we have seen our Iraqi Christian family express a similar perspective. They are convinced that God is doing something bigger than what they are suffering, and they want to be faithful to fulfill their part in God's work.

What have you learned from them about seeing God's perspective when you are persecuted and suffer at the hands of others?

How important is our willingness to forgive in the big picture of what God is accomplishing?

Sometimes we are unwilling to forgive because we want "justice" for those who have wronged us. What does Romans 12:14, 17–20 tell us about seeking justice?

Bless those who persecute you; bless and do not curse them.… Repay no one evil for evil, but give thought to do what is honorable in the sight of all. If possible, so far as it depends on you, live peaceably

with all. Beloved, never avenge yourselves, but leave
it to the wrath of God, for it is written, "Vengeance
is mine, I will repay, says the Lord." To the contrary,
"if your enemy is hungry, feed him; if he is thirsty,
give him something to drink; for by so doing you
will heap burning coals on his head."

How important is forgiveness in blessing others, doing what is honorable, and living peaceably without revenge?

In what ways does our willingness to forgive our enemies exemplify
1 Peter 3:9: "Do not repay evil for evil or reviling for reviling, but on
the contrary, bless, for to this you were called"?

If we are committed to following Jesus faithfully, we must forgive
as he forgives. Perhaps the greatest blessing we can give to someone
who does not know Jesus, to someone who persecutes us because we
follow Jesus, is to forgive. Forgiveness advances God's kingdom. It is
what God wants for us and for those who do not know him.

Who has God put you in a position to bless by offering forgiveness
for wrongs committed against you?

Will you forgive that person?

Faithfulness

*Therefore, my beloved brothers, be steadfast, immovable,
always abounding in the work of the Lord, knowing
that in the Lord your labor is not in vain.*

1 Corinthians 15:58

Session Start-Up

Anyone who follows Jesus and serves him faithfully will pay a price. It doesn't matter if we live in a community controlled by Islamic extremists who expel or kill everyone who follows Jesus or in a community where we have the political right to practice our faith but are social pariahs if we do so. Jesus knew it would be this way. He knew that the evil one would tempt us to doubt God, to fear our circumstances, to choose the easy path over the difficult one, and ultimately to deny Jesus and abandon our walk with him.

It is not easy to be faithful when:

Teaching our family, friends, and neighbors about
Jesus can cost us our lives.

Worshipping with our fellow believers invites wholesale slaughter by Islamic militants.

Holding fast to our faith in Jesus and refusing to pledge allegiance to any other name results in beatings, rape, torture, imprisonment, or death.

Standing for the truth of what God says in his Word leads to scorn, hatred, and exclusion from our communities because it is not politically correct.

Yet God calls everyone who commits to follow him to be faithful despite the forces that oppose us. In today's video, we will meet persecuted followers of Jesus who live on the edge of survival and faithfully serve him. It is amazing to see their trust and joy in God's faithfulness even though they live in a terrible situation and the ISIS forces that drove them from their homes are only sixty miles away. How do they do it? They walk faithfully in the strength of their relationship with the great and powerful God who is present with us, will do all that he promises, and will reward us for all eternity. Let's see how they choose to serve God faithfully every day as they focus, trust, and rely on him.

Prayer

Dear Lord, when we are persecuted for our faith in you, we sometimes are tempted to doubt your goodness and to question your faithfulness. Sometimes we are afraid to stand up for you. Forgive us for our lack of love and trust in you. Thank you for always being faithful to us. For hearing our prayers. For guiding us down paths we can't even imagine. Today, during this final session, please show us how to stand faithfully for you and how to be faithful to our persecuted family so that they realize they are not alone. In your name we pray, Jesus, amen.

Video Exploration
Video Notes

> The challenge of keeping people alive
>
> God, our Father, is working miracles
>
> We lost everything, but we found Jesus
>
> Standing together as one

Video Discussion

1. As you began to see the daily living situation and faithfulness of your displaced Christian brothers and sisters in Iraq, what touched your heart, and why?

Do you think the Christians interviewed in this video find it easy to be faithful to God in their present circumstances? Why or why not?

In what ways does their example of faithfulness contribute to your understanding of what it means to be faithful to Christ?

2. What are your thoughts about the miraculous way God protected the church from bomb attacks?

What do you think the church pastor has discovered about God's faithfulness, and what impact has it had on him?

In what ways does his enthusiasm for serving Christ faithfully encourage you to be faithful?

3. What do you think enables a person to say "I have lost everything" and yet be thankful because of what it led to in that person's relationship with Jesus?

4. What stands out in your mind as you think about the faithfulness of these Christians?

5. What one thing would you want to share with these faithful believers?

Bible Perspective

In Iraq, Syria, and many other places where Islamic militants have seized power, faithfulness comes at a high price for our brothers and sisters in Christ. Yet Jesus followers who face these threats remain faithful. They continue to be identified with Jesus and to pursue his calling to do good and tell others about him. We are able to be faithful in these ways only as we focus on, trust in, and rely on God. Let's see what the Bible teaches us about the faithfulness of God who alone is our refuge and strength. Let's see how we can encourage one another to be faithful to all that God has called us to be.

1. After Israel had been unfaithful to God by demanding an earthly king, Samuel instructed them in faithfulness:

> Yet do not turn aside from following the LORD, but serve the LORD with all your heart. And do not turn aside after empty things that cannot profit or deliver, for they are empty. For the LORD will not forsake his people, for his great name's sake, because it has pleased the LORD to make you a people for himself. Moreover, as for me, far be it from me that I should sin against the LORD by ceasing to pray for you, and I will instruct you in the good and the right way. Only fear the LORD and serve him faithfully with all your heart. For consider what great things he has done for you. (1 Samuel 12:20–24)

Which parts of Samuel's instruction do you find particularly helpful in understanding how to be faithful in our walk with God?

Which parts of this instruction do you think are particularly helpful for our persecuted family in Christ?

How can we better serve our brothers and sisters in Christ and encourage them to be faithful in the midst of the persecution they endure?

2. In our Western culture, we are inclined to think that *we* make ourselves faithful to God. According to Galatians 2:20, however, "I

have been crucified with Christ. It is no longer I who live, but Christ who lives in me. And the life I now live in the flesh I live by faith in the Son of God, who loved me and gave himself for me." And 5:22 continues, "But the fruit of the Spirit is love, joy, peace, patience, kindness, goodness, faithfulness." What is the Bible's perspective on our source of faithfulness, and why is it important to recognize?

3. There is no doubt that our persecuted brothers and sisters in Iraq (as well as in other locations) face great risks in remaining faithful to God and laboring to advance his kingdom. First Peter 4:19 tells believers how to face those risks: "Therefore let those who suffer according to God's will entrust their souls to a faithful Creator while doing good." What assurance does this provide for those who seek to serve Christ?

Peter continues his advice for those who desire to serve Christ faithfully in 1 Peter 5:6–10:

> Humble yourselves, therefore, under the mighty hand of God so that at the proper time he may exalt you, casting all your anxieties on him, because he cares for you. Be sober-minded; be watchful. Your adversary the devil prowls around like a roaring lion, seeking someone to devour. Resist him, firm in your faith, knowing that the same kinds of suffering are being experienced by your brotherhood throughout the world. And after you have suffered a little while, the God of all grace, who has called you

to his eternal glory in Christ, will himself restore, confirm, strengthen, and establish you.

The Bible does not "sugarcoat" the reality of serving Christ faithfully. What hope does God offer to those who risk everything for him, and what do you think that hope means to our persecuted family in Iraq in light of the challenges and risks they face as they serve God?

4. Paul explains his motivation for risking everything for his Lord and Savior in Acts 20:22–24: "And now, behold, I am going to Jerusalem, constrained by the Spirit, not knowing what will happen to me there, except that the Holy Spirit testifies to me in every city that imprisonment and afflictions await me. But I do not account my life of any value nor as precious to myself, if only I may finish my course and the ministry that I received from the Lord Jesus, to testify to the gospel of the grace of God."

In what ways have we seen this motivation lived out by our persecuted family in Iraq?

In what ways is this like, or unlike, our motivation to serve Jesus?

What might an "unstoppable" commitment to serve Jesus look like in our communities?

5. Our persecuted brothers and sisters face overwhelming odds as they seek to advance God's kingdom, but God does not send

them—or us—into the battle ill-prepared. Read the following two passages, then answer the questions that follow:

> I give thanks to my God always for you because of the grace of God that was given you in Christ Jesus, that in every way you were enriched in him in all speech and all knowledge—even as the testimony about Christ was confirmed among you—so that you are not lacking in any gift, as you wait for the revealing of our Lord Jesus Christ, who will sustain you to the end, guiltless in the day of our Lord Jesus Christ. God is faithful, by whom you were called into the fellowship of his Son, Jesus Christ our Lord. (1 Corinthians 1:4–9)

> But as for you, continue in what you have learned and have firmly believed, knowing from whom you learned it and how from childhood you have been acquainted with the sacred writings, which are able to make you wise for salvation through faith in Christ Jesus. All Scripture is breathed out by God and profitable for teaching, for reproof, for correction, and for training in righteousness, that the man of God may be complete, equipped for every good work. (2 Timothy 3:14–17)

What assurance does God provide for those who labor faithfully to accomplish his work, no matter how challenging the circumstances may be?

What comfort and encouragement does God's faithful equipping and grace provide for us as we seek to accomplish the work he has set before us?

6. We are tempted to think that we must know the right timing, have the extra resources, the right reputation, or good health in order to serve God faithfully. But 2 Corinthians 6:2–10 provides a much different perspective:

> Behold, now is the favorable time; behold, now is the day of salvation. We put no obstacle in anyone's way, so that no fault may be found with our ministry, but as servants of God we commend ourselves in every way: by great endurance, in afflictions, hardships, calamities, beatings, imprisonments, riots, labors, sleepless nights, hunger; by purity, knowledge, patience, kindness, the Holy Spirit, genuine love; by truthful speech, and the power of God; with the weapons of righteousness for the right hand and for the left; through honor and dishonor, through slander and praise. We are treated as impostors, and yet are true; as unknown, and yet well known; as dying, and behold, we live; as punished, and yet not killed; as sorrowful, yet always rejoicing; as poor, yet making many rich; as having nothing, yet possessing everything.

When is the right time to serve God faithfully, and what do we need in order to do it?

When we think of our persecuted family in Iraq, most of whom have had everything taken from them, or have given up all they had in order to diligently serve God, how do you think this passage encourages them?

> Once, the guard showed me a food parcel. He told me it contained chocolate and other good things (from VOM). It was not given to me, but it was an encouragement to know that my friends cared about me. That fact meant more than the food. On another occasion, I was told that ten parcels had arrived for me from Norway, but I was not given these either ... it is a great joy for us to experience definite spiritual fellowship with Christians in different parts of the world. This gave us hope in prison. I want to send an expression of love from us all to those who have cared about us and prayed for us.
>
> Aida Skripnikova

Our Response

As followers of Jesus, we have the great privilege of pursuing and serving God not just as individuals but as a family, as the body of Christ. In fact, being a faithful Christian is not meant to be a solitary endeavor. God created us to serve him faithfully and to support and encourage one another toward that end *together*.

Each of us has an important role in helping one another to remain faithful—focused on doing what God says is right and reminding each other of his faithfulness. Hebrews 10:23–25 describes this encouragement: "Let us hold fast the confession of our hope without wavering, for he who promised is faithful. And let us consider how to stir up one another to love and good works, not neglecting to meet together … but encouraging one another, and all the more as you see the Day drawing near."

When we remain faithful, we inspire others to remain faithful—to focus their hearts and minds on Jesus, to face the temptations, to endure persecution, to risk everything to follow him. So we each must ask:

Am I willing to be faithful to stand with my persecuted family in Christ throughout the world—especially in areas dominated by Muslim extremists—who tenaciously cling to God and trust him to empower them to remain faithful no matter how high the cost?

Am I willing to join my brothers and sisters to be "n"?

It is no small thing to stand united with the body of Christ in faithful service to God and in support of one another. Notice what Ephesians 2:19–22 says about the family of God: "So then you are no longer strangers and aliens, but you are fellow citizens with the saints and members of the household of God, built on the foundation of the apostles and prophets, Christ Jesus himself being the cornerstone, in whom the whole structure, being joined together, grows into a holy temple in the Lord. In him you also are being built together into a dwelling place for God by the Spirit."

What does our solidarity with the body of Christ create, and why is this important in a world that is plagued by evil?

According to Philippians 1:3–6, what privilege and hope do we have when we are partners together in God's work? "I thank my God in all my remembrance of you, always in every prayer of mine for you all making my prayer with joy, because of your partnership in the gospel from the first day until now. And I am sure of this, that he who began a good work in you will bring it to completion at the day of Jesus Christ."

How can we be partners in the gospel with our persecuted brothers and sisters in Christ?

What specific things can we pray for, and what can we do to support our fellow believers?

Closing Prayer

Dear Lord, we thank you for the time we have had to come before you and learn about the persecution our Christian family is experiencing at the hands of Islamic extremists. We ache for them in their suffering. We are blessed by their faithfulness. We are excited by the ways they are accomplishing your work on earth. May we be willing and faithful partners with them. May our stand for you be so strong that we too will be labeled "n." In Jesus's name we pray, amen.

If you are a Christian, you will suffer. That is the gospel. So, pray for the brother and sister around the world, for the suffering around the world, because one day you will need them, you need their voice. I know they will be praying for you when the time comes.

A Voice of the Martyrs national contact

Next Steps
Encouragement to Remain Faithful

There are many ways we can demonstrate our faithfulness to God and his calling to advance the gospel. Romans 12:9–21 gives us quite a list. As you read these instructions and examples, consider 1) the practical ways you can live out your faithfulness to God as you go about your daily life; 2) how your persecuted brothers and sisters in Christ have demonstrated their faithfulness in these areas; 3) how faithfulness shown in these areas encourages other believers to remain strong in the Lord.

Let love be genuine. Abhor what is evil; hold fast to what is good. Love one another with brotherly affection. Outdo one another in showing honor. Do not be slothful in zeal, be fervent in spirit, serve the Lord. Rejoice in hope, be patient in tribulation, be constant in prayer. Contribute to the needs of the saints and seek to show hospitality.

Bless those who persecute you; bless and do not curse them. Rejoice with those who rejoice, weep with those who weep. Live in harmony with one another. Do not be haughty, but associate with the lowly. Never be wise in your own sight. Repay no one evil for evil, but give thought to do what is honorable in the sight of all. If possible, so far as it depends on you, live peaceably with all. Beloved, never avenge yourselves, but leave it to the wrath of God, for it is written, "Vengeance is mine, I will repay, says the Lord." To the contrary, "if your enemy is hungry, feed him; if he is thirsty, give him something to drink; for by so doing you will heap burning coals on his head." Do not be overcome by evil, but overcome evil with good.

When Paul was in chains he wrote, "What has happened to me has really served to advance the gospel." Because of Paul's fearless faithfulness, "most of the brothers ... in the Lord ... are much more bold to speak the word without fear" (Philippians 1:12, 14).

What happened to Jesus followers when the apostle Paul was in chains is happening all over the world today! Islamic extremists are not just persecuting Christians in Iraq and Syria. It is not just ISIS; it is Boko Haram, Al-Shabab, the Taliban, Fulani, and many more. It is happening in Nigeria, Iran, Somalia, Pakistan, Turkey, and the Philippines, just to name a few. When one persecuted Christian remains faithful to God, it affects other Jesus followers. The faithfulness of one inspires others to remain true to God—to focus their hearts and minds on Jesus and face the temptations, endure the persecution, and risk everything to follow him. Will you stand with them?

Our Persecuted Family around the World

The map on the following pages shows countries where Christians are persecuted for their faith in Jesus. In most of these countries, persecution comes from Islamic extremists. Read the sampling of profiles of our Christian brothers and sisters who have been persecuted by such groups and ask yourself if you also will be faithful.

Pray for the Persecuted (a key for the map)

● *RESTRICTED*

This includes countries where government-sanctioned circumstances or anti-Christian laws lead to Christians being harassed, imprisoned, killed, or deprived of possessions or liberties because of their witness. Also included are countries where government policy or practice prevents Christians from obtaining Bibles or other Christian literature.

● *HOSTILE*

This includes nations or large areas of nations where governments consistently attempt to provide protection for the Christian population but where Christians are routinely persecuted by family, friends, neighbors, or political groups because of their witness.

● *MONITORED*

These are areas being closely monitored by VOM because of a trend toward increased persecution of Christians. The frequency and severity of persecution do not currently meet the criteria of the Hostile category.

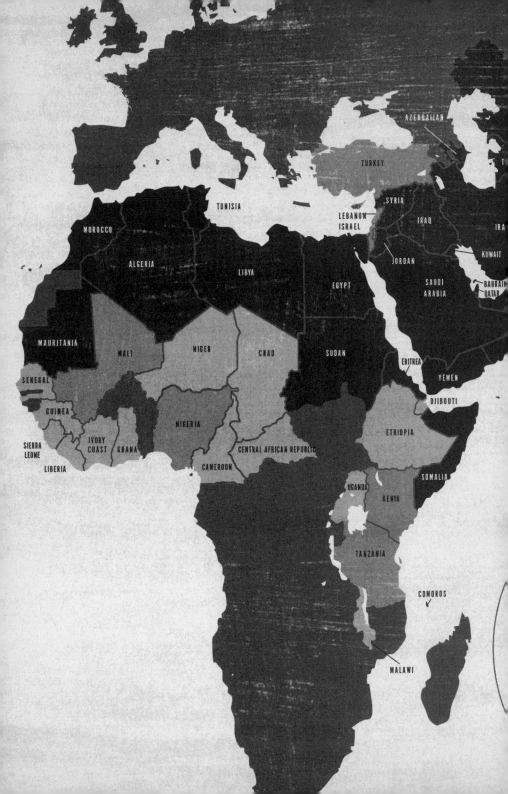

Egypt—Naasir and Hoda

"Happily-ever-afters" are not common among Jesus followers in Egypt. That did not deter Naasir and Hoda. They fell in love, married, and vowed to do everything they could do to share their faith in Christ with others. But it would not be easy for them.

Muslims often harassed and mocked them. Landlords evicted them when they learned of their Christian faith. After a move to yet another apartment, their furniture fell apart. They had no food. The weather turned cold. They slept on the floor. It was hardly the stable living situation they wanted for their young son. But all of this they endured gladly in order to remain faithful to their calling.

Today Naasir is an evangelist who teaches others how to share God's Word. Hoda spearheads a ministry to shelter women in Cairo who have been evicted from their homes after converting to Christianity. "We have had many chances to leave Egypt," Hoda says, "but we are convinced that we have to be in Egypt to complete our ministry here."

Nigeria—Danjuma

Early on that terrible day, gunshots jolted Danjuma awake. Like everyone else in his small village, he ran for his life. But escape from the attack by nearly one thousand Islamic insurgents proved impossible for the thirteen-year-old boy.

Danjuma remembers all too well the pain of a machete slicing through the left side of his head. But he recalls nothing, thankfully, of what happened next. Not the machete blows to his left arm. Not the gouging out of his eye with a knife. Not the continuous torture. He vaguely remembers the disbelief and excitement of the men who had been digging his grave when they realized he was still alive!

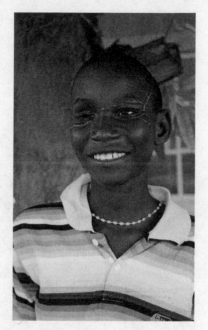

The staff at the hospital where Danjuma was taken could not believe he was alive. "He bled so much. It is a miracle," a hospital manager said.

Now Danjuma, the boy with the peaceful smile, has the nickname "Miracle," not only because he lived, but because he feels less sorry for himself than for those who maimed him. "I forgive them because they don't know what they are doing," he said, echoing words he had read in the Bible. "If they had love, they wouldn't behave that way."

Gaza City—Pauline and Rami

Managing a bookstore doesn't seem like a high-risk occupation—unless it is a Christian bookstore in Gaza City, a Muslim-dominated city of half a million people in the Gaza Strip. The store served about thirty-five hundred Palestinian Christians, but it was in Hamas territory where the Christian faith is viewed as a threat. That made store manager Rami Ayyad's work dangerous.

Pauline, Rami's wife, was a young mother of two with a third child on the way. She knew Islamic extremists threatened the store regularly. They had bombed it twice. But Rami remained steadfast in his belief that he was doing the right thing by working there. "Jesus is the love of my life," he told her, "and I will never deny him, regardless of what happens."

One day, Pauline received a panicked phone call from Rami telling her that three Islamic fundamentalists had come into the store.

She never heard her husband speak again. The next morning, his bullet-ridden, knife-scarred body was found near the store.

Pauline felt as if she, too, had been stabbed and shot to death. Her pain wouldn't go away. For a time, she says she "hated Muslims, hated everybody." But as she received support, encouragement, and prayer from Jesus followers around the world, she began a long journey toward forgiveness. Years after Rami's death, she realized the life-changing truth that the Muslims who killed her husband were the very ones she and other Christians needed to reach for Jesus!

The Philippines—Armando and Ruth

Armando, Ruth, and their three children ran through the darkness. They huddled together in the only place that could conceal them, underneath a footbridge in shallow water frequented by poisonous snakes. Frightened, the children cried. "You must be quiet," Ruth whispered, "very, very quiet."

For the next eight hours, the couple whispered encouragement to their children and prayed for protection for their family and ministry. Until that night, their village had not been attacked by Islamist fighters active on the island of Mindanao. The next morning, they crawled out of their hiding place, hurriedly gathered a few belongings, and disappeared into the jungle with other villagers who survived the attack. Nightfall, they knew, would bring more fighting.

For several weeks, they camped in the dark jungle thick with bamboo, ferns, and banana trees. For the next five years, rebels were so often near the village that residents adapted a new routine. They would stay in the village and tend livestock and gardens during the day. At night they would leave to sleep in makeshift tents hidden in the jungle.

Through all the hardship and risk, Ruth and Armando stayed to raise their children and to remain faithful to the work God had for them. "There is a big work in this place," Ruth said. "Let us continue to serve the Lord even though experiencing this kind of persecution. All these things are happening to us, but God is still great.... God has called us here. If we die, we *die*."

Iran—Hussein

By age seventeen, Hussein was a full-fledged drug addict, but he was hungry for something more. He found what he was looking for when he committed his life to Jesus. His desire for drugs faded. His life turned from hopeless to hopeful, from lost to saved, from death to life.

But in Iran, these changes caused some people to want to snuff out the hope of Jesus. Not only did Hussein's Muslim father report him to the authorities in hopes that his "apostate" son would be arrested, he promised to "be the one who'll put the rope around your neck" if they decided to hang Hussein.

Hussein was arrested but not hanged. He was handed over to prison guards who carried out their own justice. Hussein wanted to stand for Jesus; they broke one of his legs. Hussein wanted to praise God with music; they broke all his fingers. Hussein wanted to bow before Christ in humility; they ripped open his back with forty lashes from a whip.

With each sacrifice required of him—his leg, his hands, his back—he continued to honor God and tell others about him. Despite his suffering, he wrote: "None of these punishments made me upset, except that I cannot play music for the Lord now."

How will you stand with the men, women, and children who tenaciously cling to the hope that God will empower them to remain faithful despite the evil done to them?

Will you support them in prayer? Will you help to provide for their needs? Will you share their stories with others, perhaps leading an i-am-n study in your church or community?

The commitment statement at the end of this book will help you connect with practical ways to encourage your family in Christ to remain faithful.

We will not let our brothers and sisters suffer in silence, nor will we let them serve alone.

I Am N Commitment Prayer

Heavenly Father,

I have been inspired by my persecuted Christian brothers and sisters, and I ask that you will empower me to take active steps so I can grow in:

SACRIFICE. I will count the cost of discipleship and willingly pay the price because you are worth it.

COURAGE. I will not be paralyzed by fear because you empower me as I take risks to witness for you.

JOY. I will rejoice in the midst of my struggles and suffering in this world because of the eternal hope I have in you.

PERSEVERANCE. I will stand firm, resisting any opposition. By your strength, I will endure and overcome.

FORGIVENESS. I will allow you to work in my heart as I obey you by loving my enemies and forgiving others as you have forgiven me.

FAITHFULNESS. I will not allow adversity to cause me to be unfaithful to your Word or disobedient to your purposes.

Lord, help me be mindful of my Christian family so I will never let my Christian brothers and sisters suffer in silence, nor will I let them serve alone. I will let their testimonies inspire me to follow you. *I am n.*

_____   _____

Name   Date

www.i-am-n.com

Are You an "N" Christian?

To learn more about your persecuted family members and to get your church involved, go to *www.i-am-n.com/products*.

i am n

the voice of the martyrs

i am n

David C Cook®

transforming lives together

I AM N PARTICIPANT'S GUIDE
Published by David C Cook
4050 Lee Vance View
Colorado Springs, CO 80918 U.S.A.

David C Cook U.K., Kingsway Communications
Eastbourne, East Sussex BN23 6NT, England

The graphic circle C logo is a registered trademark of David C Cook.

The website addresses recommended throughout this book are offered as a
resource to you. These websites are not intended in any way to be or imply an
endorsement on the part of David C Cook, nor do we vouch for their content.

Unless otherwise noted, all Scripture quotations are taken from the ESV®
Bible (The Holy Bible, English Standard Version®), copyright © 2001
by Crossway, a publishing ministry of Good News Publishers. Used by
permission. All rights reserved. Scripture quotations marked KJV are
taken from the King James Version of the Bible. (Public Domain.)

Details in some stories have been changed to protect
the identities of the persons involved.

LCCN 2015958975
ISBN 978-1-4347-1002-4
eISBN 978-1-4347-1040-6

© 2016 The Voice of the Martyrs, Inc.

Printed in the United States of America
First Edition 2016

3 4 5 6 7 8 9 10

050316